Matthew Cappucci
Illustrated by **Stephanie Hathaway**

# EXTREME WEATHER for Kids

## LESSONS AND ACTIVITIES ALL ABOUT HURRICANES, TORNADOES, BLIZZARDS, AND MORE!

QUARRY

**Quarto.com**

© 2024 Quarto Publishing Group USA Inc.
Text © 2024 Matthew Cappucci

First Published in 2024 by Quarry Books, an imprint of The Quarto Group,
100 Cummings Center, Suite 265-D, Beverly, MA 01915, USA.
T (978) 282-9590 F (978) 283-2742

Quarry Books titles are also available at discount for retail, wholesale, promotional, and bulk purchase. For details, contact the Special Sales Manager by email at specialsales@quarto.com or by mail at The Quarto Group, Attn: Special Sales Manager, 100 Cummings Center, Suite 265-D, Beverly, MA 01915, USA.

10 9 8 7 6 5 4 3 2 1

ISBN: 978-0-7603-8514-2

Digital edition published in 2024
eISBN: 978-0-7603-8515-9

Library of Congress Cataloging-in-Publication Data is available.


Design and Page Layout: Mattie Wells Design
Cover Illustration: Stephanie Hathaway
Cover Images: Adobe Stock and Shutterstock (top row) and Adobe Stock (bottom row)
Photography: Matthew Cappucci unless otherwise noted
Illustration: Stephanie Hathaway

Printed in China

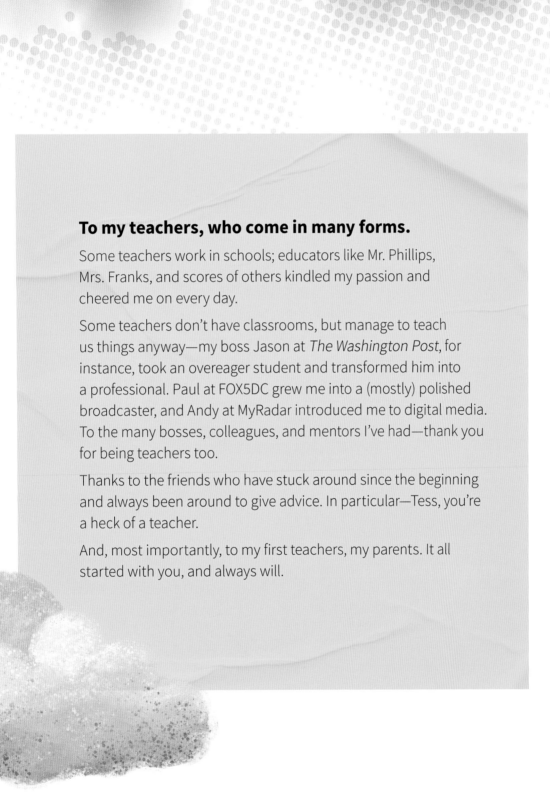

**To my teachers, who come in many forms.**

Some teachers work in schools; educators like Mr. Phillips, Mrs. Franks, and scores of others kindled my passion and cheered me on every day.

Some teachers don't have classrooms, but manage to teach us things anyway—my boss Jason at *The Washington Post*, for instance, took an overeager student and transformed him into a professional. Paul at FOX5DC grew me into a (mostly) polished broadcaster, and Andy at MyRadar introduced me to digital media. To the many bosses, colleagues, and mentors I've had—thank you for being teachers too.

Thanks to the friends who have stuck around since the beginning and always been around to give advice. In particular—Tess, you're a heck of a teacher.

And, most importantly, to my first teachers, my parents. It all started with you, and always will.

# CONTENTS

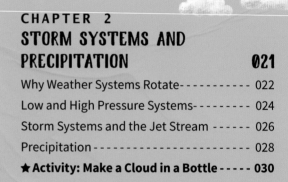

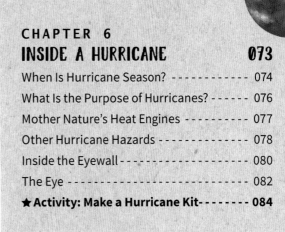

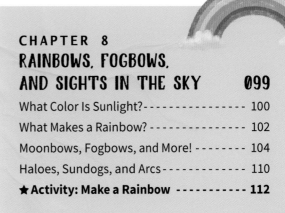

# INTRODUCTION

**H**iya gang! Welcome to *Extreme Weather for Kids*. If you've ever been curious about what's going on in the skies above, you're in luck! We're here to answer your questions—and hopefully spark a few more.

Weather affects everyone. No matter who you are or where you live, the weather is important. Most of the time, the weather is well-behaved. But sometimes, extreme storms occur. Big storms can be both scary and exciting at the same time. Our goal with this book is to understand why they exist, how they form, and how we can stay safe.

We also want to pursue our natural curiosities! It's important to be curious about the world around us. Have you ever wondered why the sky is blue? Can triple rainbows exist? How hot is lightning? And can wildfires really spawn tornadoes? We'll investigate the answers to these questions and more, picking up some useful knowledge along the way.

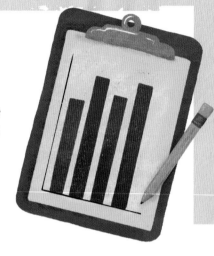

This book will feature key lessons delivered in a way that makes complex scientific topics accessible to anyone. We'll also bring these lessons to life through a combination of Storm Chase Adventures stories and hands-on experiments and activities woven throughout our lessons.

Every Storm Chase Adventures story will tell about a real-life example of extreme weather in action. Some of the activities will re-create weather processes to demonstrate concepts. Others will teach lessons on how to take and interpret observations. Together, the different elements of *Extreme Weather for Kids* are sure to capture the true excitement and dynamics of the atmosphere we all share.

Above all, our goal is simple—to be inspired to look up! The atmosphere is nature's biggest classroom. The skies constantly put on shows of physics for us to decipher. All we have to do is pay attention.

A potent supercell, or rotating thunderstorm, casts an eerie green hue on the morning sky near Colby, Kansas, USA on May 26, 2021. (Matthew Cappucci)

Meteorologist Matthew Cappucci (left) in the Azores, an area of nine volcanic islands in the mid-Atlantic Ocean and (right) at work in front of the green screen, sharing the day's weather forecast.

A display of mammatus (pouch-like) clouds reminiscent of bubble wrapping on May 12, 2018, near Elk City, Oklahoma, USA. The clouds hang beneath the anvil of a severe thunderstorm. (Matthew Cappucci)

## CHAPTER 1:

# PREDICTING THE WEATHER

Have you ever wondered what makes a hurricane? Or how a tornado spins so fast? Or why snowflakes have six sides? And which comes first—lightning or thunder? From 10-foot (3-meter) snowfall to hailstorms with chunks of ice the size of bowling balls, simple ingredients—just air, water, and heat—can combine into extraordinary displays of raw power and beauty. Earth's weather can be absolutely wild.

Weather is defined as the state of the **atmosphere**, the envelope of air that surrounds the Earth. Sometimes, the weather is calm and beautiful. Other times, the weather can be in a *really* bad mood. That's why there's an entire field dedicated to studying the weather, known as **meteorology**.

A **meteorologist** is a scientist who researches and predicts the weather. Weather forecasts are useful to everyone. Families rely on weather forecasts to plan their days and stay safe. Airline pilots and ship captains monitor weather forecasts to plot their routes. And even candy companies hire meteorologists—after all, the crops needed to produce chocolate depend heavily on the weather!

Obviously, the weather is important—especially during major storms and extreme weather. So buckle up! In this chapter, we'll learn what drives Earth's weather, starting with what makes the seasons. This chapter also explores how meteorologists observe weather and make predictions.

So what are you waiting for? Let's dive into Mother Nature's wildest storms.

Today's Weather
77°F

Mon 82°F · Tues 74°F · Wed 76°F

# WHAT MAKES THE WEATHER?

**M**ost weather occurs in the lowest layer of the atmosphere. It's made up mostly of nitrogen, but also contains oxygen—what we breathe—argon, and other gases.

All weather is driven by the transfer of heat, also known as **thermal energy**.

But the sun doesn't deliver heat to everywhere on Earth equally—some places see more sunshine, and others receive less. That uneven heating drives air currents—or movements of air. Those processes are what make weather systems.

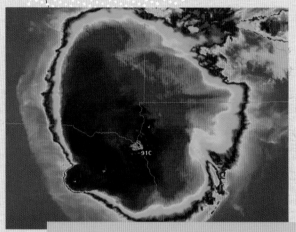

↑ A storm complex over the central United States. (UW-CIMSS)

## WHAT ARE SEASONS?

We all know *what* the seasons are—winter, spring, summer, and fall—but *why* do they occur? It's all due to Earth's tilt on its axis.

An **axis** is an imaginary line that a spinning object rotates around. Earth rotates on its axis once every 24 hours. This gives us day or night, depending on if we're facing toward or away from the sun.

All the while, Earth **orbits**, or circles around, the sun once every year. Because Earth's axis is tilted 23.5 degrees, different parts of the planet get more sunlight during certain points of its annual orbit.

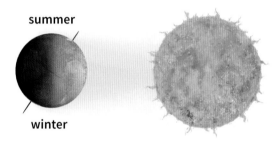

summer

winter

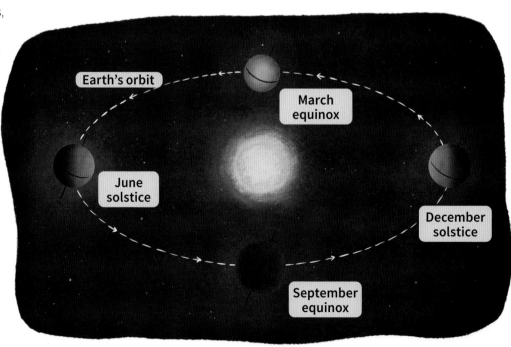

Earth's orbit

March equinox

June solstice

December solstice

September equinox

## SUMMER AND WINTER

Summer occurs when one **hemisphere**, or half of the world, is tilted toward the sun. The Northern Hemisphere, where North America, Europe, and Asia are located, is pointed most directly at the sun in June. For them, that's called the **summer solstice**.

That's precisely when South America, Australia, and Antarctica—located in the Southern Hemisphere—are leaning *away* from the sun. They're simultaneously experiencing their **winter solstice**.

Six months later, in December, the opposite happens. The Southern Hemisphere basks in the sun's most direct rays and experiences its summer solstice. That means that Christmas, Hanukkah, and New Year's are *summer* holidays there. Meanwhile, the Northern Hemisphere shivers. It's their winter solstice.

→ A composite photograph of the sun's position at noontime over the course of the year. The image was made by combining photos from the 1998–1999 season in Murray Hill, New Jersey, USA. (Wikipedia/Jfishburn)

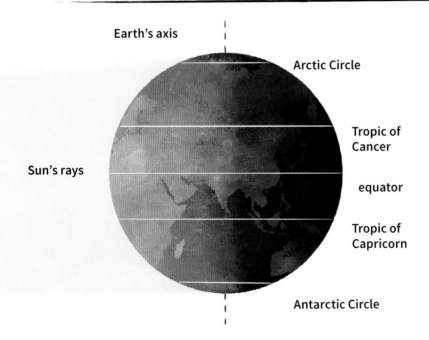

Earth's axis

Arctic Circle

Tropic of Cancer

equator

Sun's rays

Tropic of Capricorn

Antarctic Circle

## TRANSITION SEASONS: SPRING AND FALL

Twice a year in our orbit around the sun, Earth reaches a point where *neither* hemisphere is aimed more toward the sun. This is called an **equinox**. There's one in late March and one in late September. The equinoxes mark the first day of spring and fall.

On the equinox, the sun's most direct rays shine over the equator. Every location on Earth experiences an approximate equal length of day and night.

### DID YOU KNOW?

The amount and intensity of sunlight an area receives directly influences the weather. Longer days with more intense solar heating bring warmer weather. Shorter days or indirect sunlight translates to colder weather.

# THE LAND OF THE MIDNIGHT SUN

Imagine the sun not setting for 100 days! Or a night that's *months* long. That's reality for **polar** regions, or parts of the world near the North Pole or South Pole. The polar regions are defined as locations within about 23.5 degrees of each pole. In the Northern Hemisphere, that's everything north of an invisible line called the **Arctic Circle**. In the Southern Hemisphere, it's called the **Antarctic Circle**.

If you're in either the Arctic or Antarctic, you'll have at least one day per year where the sun skims along the horizon for 24 hours and a minimum of one day where the sun *never* rises. The farther poleward, or toward the poles, you go, the more extreme the annual variation.

Utqiaġvik, Alaska, formerly known as Barrow, is the northernmost town in the United States. It's home to about 5,000 people. Temperatures can hover near or below freezing from October through May and plummet as low as minus (-) 50 degrees Fahrenheit (°F), or minus (-) 46 degrees Celsius (°C), in the dead of winter. During the wintertime, Utqiaġvik goes two months without seeing the sun! But in the summer, the sun goes 81 days without setting.

Because the air is so cold, it holds little moisture. That means it doesn't rain or snow much in Utqiaġvik. The community only averages 5.39 inches (13.7 cm) of precipitation per year. That means Utqiaġvik is a desert!

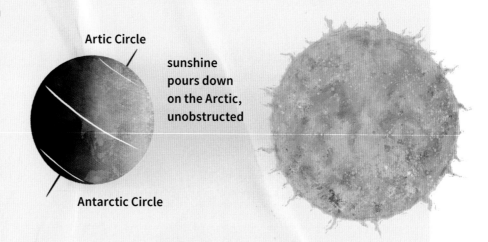

Artic Circle

sunshine pours down on the Arctic, unobstructed

Antarctic Circle

↑ A view of Utqiaġvik, Alaska, on August 17, 2007. (Dave Cohoe)

# HOW METEOROLOGISTS PREDICT THE WEATHER

**M**aking weather forecasts is just like making predictions about anything else. In order to guess what *will* happen in a system, you need to know two things:

**What's happening now.** Scientists call this **initial conditions**. It's like driving—in order to map out where you're *going*, you need to first know where you are now!

**The rules of how the system behaves.** You need to understand how different parts of the system interact with and influence one another.

In the world of weather, initial conditions take the form of weather **observations**. What is the weather like now? What's the temperature? How humid is it? Is it raining? Meteorologists have devised lots of ways to observe what is happening in the present.

For what comes *next*, meteorologists rely on an understanding of physics. The atmosphere can be treated like one big math problem! But the problem is so *big* that scientists need a really powerful calculator. That's where **computer models** come in.

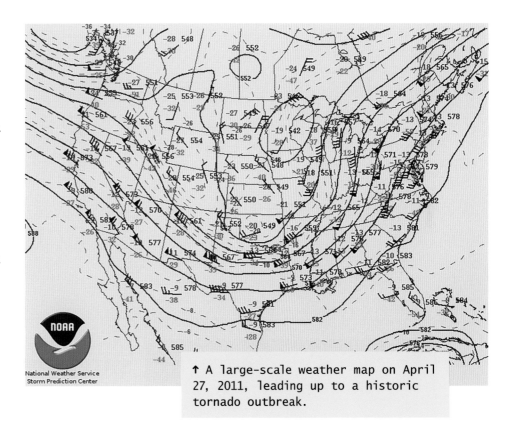

↑ A large-scale weather map on April 27, 2011, leading up to a historic tornado outbreak.

# MAKING OBSERVATIONS

Now that we've learned about what causes Earth's weather, let's explore how meteorologists predict the weather. Making predictions about what the weather will do in the *future* begins with knowing what the weather is doing *now*. Meteorologists rely on observations, or descriptions of current conditions, as a place to start.

## WEATHER STATIONS

The most direct way to gather weather data is through in-the-field weather stations. They usually consist of a metal pole with various instruments that measure temperature, dew point, relative humidity, barometric pressure, rainfall, snow accumulation, and so on. Most have wind meters called **anemometers** on the top. They record wind speed and direction.

Weather stations are often arranged in a **network**. The more weather stations in a given area, the more complete a picture a meteorologist can get, which makes for better predictions.

⚠ In Oklahoma, for example, every one of the state's 77 counties is home to at least one automated weather station. There are 120 overall that are part of a network called the Oklahoma Mesonet.

↑ An automated weather station in Colorado Springs, Colorado, USA. (NOAA)

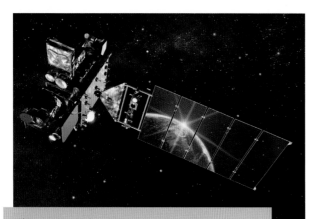

↑ An illustration of the GOES East weather satellite, which was launched in November 2016. (NOAA)

## SATELLITES

About 95 percent of the weather data that's fed into computer models comes from satellites in space. Satellites are like ultrasensitive cameras that peer down on Earth from far above. There are two main types of weather satellites:

**Geostationary** satellites orbit the Earth at the exact speed the Earth rotates. They appear fixed over the same place in our skies and survey the same areas all the time.

**Polar-orbiting** satellites are located much closer to the ground and constantly circle the Earth.

↑ A weather balloon carrying a radiosonde is being prepared for launch at a U.S. National Weather Service office. (NOAA)

## WEATHER BALLOONS

Every day, scientists around the world release balloons carrying packages of weather instruments called **radiosondes**. They measure temperature, pressure, and humidity, and that data helps meteorologists determine the current state of the atmosphere.

Weather balloons are especially helpful during thunderstorms. They allow meteorologists to deduce how much heat energy is available for storms. By measuring winds at different altitudes, weather balloons can help meteorologists predict if tornadoes are a possibility.

⚠ The balloons eventually pop, and the instrument box parachutes harmlessly down to Earth. They are designed to disintegrate if they make contact with an airplane so as to not pose any danger.

## RADARS

Weather radars are ground-based devices that can remotely sense the location and intensity of precipitation. The radar is made of a rotating antenna that spins around inside a dome. First, it emits pulses of radiation, and then it "listens" for echoes when the signal returns.

Meteorologists can also peer into clouds, looking at areas of wind and searching for possible rotation. They rely on radar signatures to issue warnings before a tornado is expected to form.

⚠ Sometimes, radar beams hit more than just rain or snow. Bugs, airplanes, buildings, butterflies, wildfire smoke, and even exploding meteors have all been spotted on weather radar!

↑ The National Weather Service radar dome located in Mount Holly, New Jersey, USA. (NOAA/NWS)

## BUOYS

Meteorologists use weather stations called **buoys** to gather data in the ocean. Buoys are floating platforms that sit on the surface of the water and rise and fall with the waves.

Most buoys measure the same attributes as land-based weather stations, but they also capture data on water temperature, wave height, and **wave period**, or how often waves roll past a location.

**⚠** On September 8, 2019, a buoy offshore of Channel-Port aux Basques, Newfoundland, measured a 100-foot (30-m) "rogue wave." Hurricane Dorian created ferocious wind gusts, causing waves to overlap and form a monstrous wall of water.

↑ A technician deploys a weather buoy. (NOAA)

↑ A WC-130J Hercules Super aircraft operated by the U.S. Air Force Reserve Hurricane Hunters. (U.S. Air Force)

## AIRCRAFT

Arguably, the most extreme type of data collection comes from **reconnaissance aircraft**—or airplanes that fly into deadly storms to take measurements. The U.S. Air Force Reserve 53rd Weather Reconnaissance Squadron, more commonly known as "The Hurricane Hunters," carries out these missions.

The Hurricane Hunters fly into the core of hurricanes and release devices called **dropsondes** out of the plane. Each one falls into the ocean below, capturing data from inside the **eyewall**.

**⚠** Hurricane hunting began during World War II, when two Army Air Corps pilots flew a single-engine North American AT-6 plane into the eye of a nearby hurricane.

# FORECASTING THE FUTURE

**M**eteorology takes *a lot* of math—like calculus and differential equations! That enables meteorologists to learn how weather systems should act. Meteorologists don't have time to do all that math, however. That's why they use **computer models**, or powerful computers that simulate the atmosphere. These computers take in initial conditions—or current observations—and are programmed to calculate what should happen next, based on the physics of the atmosphere.

↑ The European Centre for Medium-Range Weather Forecasts (ECMWF) maintains a massive supercomputer that's used to run complex dynamic weather models.

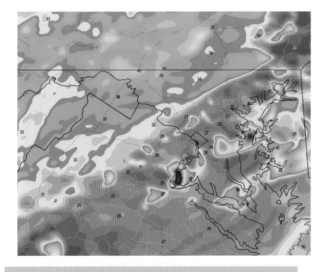

↑ A high-resolution weather model simulates wind gusts around Washington, D.C., in the United States on July 29, 2023. (WeatherBELL)

## WEATHER MODELS

Computer weather models process data, or information, from all around the world. That's a *big* task, so scientists use supercomputers. The computers break the world down into little boxes. Then, they calculate the weather in each box and stitch the answers together into virtual weather systems and storms.

Different computer models have different **resolutions**, meaning they are more or less detailed. High-resolution models can help determine weather conditions down to the minute and to a fraction of a mile, but only in the short-term.

Other long-range weather models can try to look weeks or months into the future—but their depictions are broad and not very detailed.

---

### DID YOU KNOW?

Computer models are useful, but they're not perfect. Every model has errors. Some of the errors come from not having enough observations. Others stem from imperfect programming or math. But all models are helpful in giving human forecasters a place to begin.

# MAKE A THERMOMETER

Thermometers are what meteorologists use to measure the temperature. A century ago, thermometers were made out of glass and contained liquid. That liquid would expand when it was warm or contract (shrink) when it was cold. Meteorologists could measure that effect to deduce the actual air temperature. Nowadays, most thermometers are electronic.

**Let's try making our own thermometer!**

## HERE'S WHAT YOU'LL NEED:

+ Small glass or plastic water bottle
+ Rubbing alcohol
+ Water
+ Food coloring
+ Plastic straw (a tall one that's bigger than the bottle)
+ Clay
+ Notecard
+ Pen or pencil
+ Ice
+ An adult

1. Have an adult help you pour equal parts water and rubbing alcohol into the bottle until it's about a quarter full. Squeeze a few drops of red food coloring into it.

2. Place the straw into the bottle. Then, lift it up just a bit so there's a tiny gap between the bottom of the bottle and the bottom of the straw.

3. Use clay to cover the opening of the bottle and wrap it around the straw. That will secure the straw in place. You want an airtight seal, but do not cover the hole of the straw.

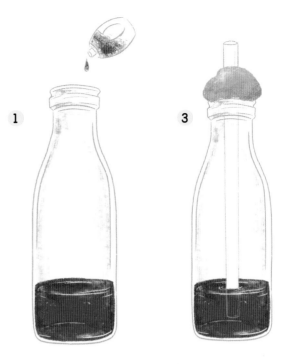

Now, your thermometer is ready! The level of the liquid inside the straw will change depending on the temperature.

Try placing your thermometer in a bowl of hot water. What happens to the liquid? Use the notecard and paper to record the height of the fluid. Now, what happens if you immerse it in a bowl of ice? Draw another line to measure the height of the red liquid.

When heated, both the air and the alcohol mixture expand. Since the container is airtight, it forces the fluid up the straw to a higher level. When cooled, the opposite occurs. The air and liquid contract and the level in the straw drops.

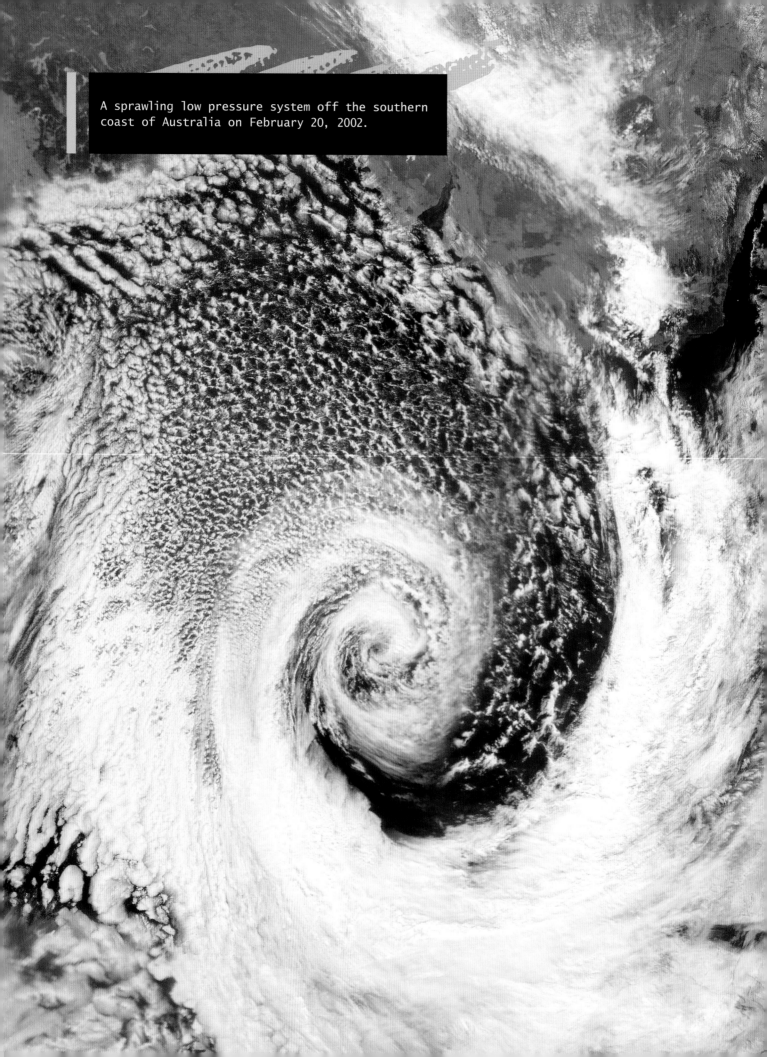

A sprawling low pressure system off the southern coast of Australia on February 20, 2002.

## CHAPTER 2

# STORM SYSTEMS AND PRECIPITATION

Though the weather may seem random and chaotic, it's actually pretty organized. Large-scale patterns dictate how storm systems behave and where they form. The biggest, most broad weather pattern is called the **general circulation**. Every weather system on the globe is affected by it.

The basics of the general circulation are simple: air rises near the equator, where it's warm, and sinks near the poles, where it's cold.

That's a simple idea, but it's made more complicated by the fact the Earth is **spinning**. That makes weather systems spin too.

In this chapter, we'll learn about **pressure systems** and how big storms form. We'll talk about the role Earth's rotation plays in the weather. And we'll find out how storm systems can make **fronts**.

# WHY WEATHER SYSTEMS ROTATE

## WHAT IS THE CORIOLIS FORCE?

The **Coriolis force** is derived from Earth's rotation.

Let's think about a merry-go-round. If you're sitting in one place, you don't notice much—but if you get up and start walking, you might feel like you're being pushed or pulled at a right angle.

Why is that? It's because *in your mind* you're walking in a straight line, but your entire *system* is rotating beneath you. On the merry-go-round, you might feel that you're tracing a curve. But someone who's not on the merry-go-round would actually see your path as straight.

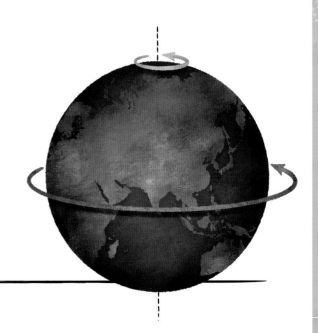

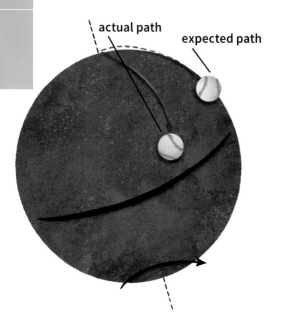

actual path

expected path

## EARTH'S SPIN AFFECTS EVERYTHING!

The northern and southern hemispheres on Earth are each like their own merry-go-round. Pretend the middle of our first merry-go-round is the North Pole, and the equator—where the radius of Earth is much wider—is the edge of the merry-go-round. If you travel anywhere between the two, you're going to experience a subtle push to the right. In the Southern Hemisphere, there's a gentle deflection to the left.

⚠ For objects that travel a long distance, the Coriolis force has to be taken into consideration. If you're flying from New York to Paris, your pilot can't just aim straight toward France. In fact, they'd have to tilt the wings about 0.15 degrees to the left to offset that rightward push of the Coriolis force.

→ Earth actually isn't a perfect sphere because it bulges outward about 27 miles (43 km) at the equator due to its spin.

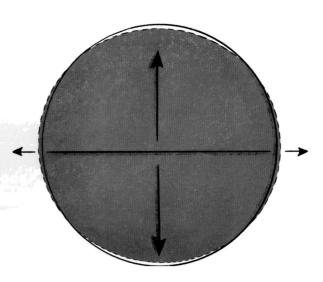

# THE EARTH AS A ROTATING SYSTEM

Let's take a look at why weather systems rotate and what kind of weather that creates. We'll also explore why weather systems spin different directions in different parts of the world.

Weather systems can span thousands of miles (kilometers) across. Because they're so large, they feel Earth's rotation and begin to rotate themselves. That means they can churn together air of different temperatures and humidities and brew lots of types of wild weather. A single storm system may contain smaller regions of snow, extreme heat, flooding rains, and even thunderstorms with tornadoes.

## ANGULAR MOMENTUM IN THE ATMOSPHERE

Have you ever tried spinning on a desk chair? If you stretch your arms out, you slow down. If you pull your arms and legs in, you speed up. (And if you hug your knees, you might spin *really* fast and get dizzy!)

That's because you have a fixed amount of **angular momentum**, or spin energy. When you stretch your limbs outward, you're using that energy to trace bigger circles, so you can't spin as fast. But when you pull your arms in, you make smaller circles, and can spin faster with the same amount of energy.

The Earth behaves a bit like that too. At the equator, the radius of Earth is the widest—about 3,959 miles (6,371 km). The equator is like the *big* circle you make when your arms are spread wide on the spinning desk chair. As you move toward the North or South Pole, however, Earth's radius shrinks.

↑ The GOES West weather satellite captures a potent low pressure system swirling off the West Coast of the United States in January of 2023. Note the counterclockwise spin. (NOAA)

## HOW THE EARTH'S ROTATION MAKES SPINNING STORMS

Things that move from the equator toward the poles move faster as the radius, or size of the circle they trace, shrinks. Because of this, they feel the impact of the Coriolis force. The Coriolis effect is strongest near the poles, where Earth's radius changes most dramatically with distance. It's weakest in the tropics and is actually zero at the equator.

The Coriolis force can cause the path of moving objects to curve. Air masses, or large bodies of air, moving long distances through the atmosphere are influenced by this force. That's what causes weather systems to spin.

# LOW AND HIGH PRESSURE SYSTEMS

## LOW PRESSURE SYSTEMS

**Low pressure systems**, or lows, are regions of rising air that often bring clouds and precipitation. As the air rises, it lifts away from the ground, leaving less atmosphere sitting on a given point. That reduces the air's weight, or **air pressure**, creating an inward pull that causes winds to flow into the low. The deeper, or stronger, the low pressure system, the faster the winds.

As the air moves inward, it curves, thanks to the Coriolis force. In the Northern Hemisphere, the air curves to the right. That makes low pressure systems spin counterclockwise. South of the equator, air curves to the left, meaning the lows spin clockwise.

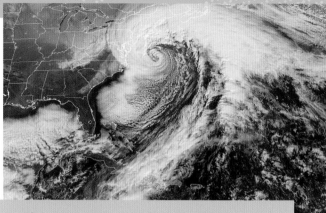

↑ The GOES East weather satellite peers down on a *bomb cyclone*, spinning off the northeast coast of the United States on January 4, 2017. (NOAA)

← A simple diagram of how low pressure systems spin on Earth.

## WHERE BIG STORM SYSTEMS CAN'T FORM

What about *on* the equator, or the invisible divider line between the two hemispheres? There, the Coriolis force is *zero*! That means you can't have a large-scale spinning weather system. There's nothing to make it spin!

That's why, despite an *enormous* amount of warm water, you can never have a hurricane form on the equator.

⚠ Storms don't cross the equator—it would have to switch the direction of its spin, which would never happen!

## HIGH PRESSURE SYSTEMS

**Highs** are the opposite. They're made of sinking air. As the descending air slowly hits the ground, it spreads outward, causing a diffusion of air. Opposite to how lows spin, highs spin clockwise in the Northern Hemisphere and counterclockwise in the Southern Hemisphere.

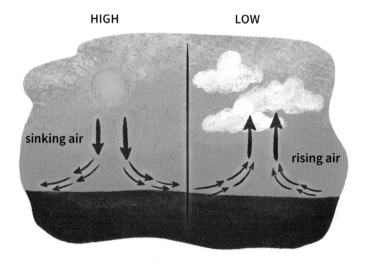

HIGH    LOW

sinking air

rising air

# THE GENERAL CIRCULATION

Now that we know about high and low pressure systems and the Coriolis force, we can put everything together. Let's discuss the **general circulation** of the atmosphere.

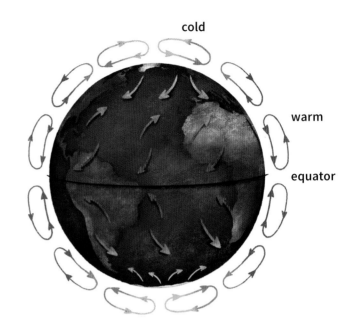

Like we talked about, warm air rises—so air pockets bubble upward at the equator where it's hot. That air ascends to the upper atmosphere, where it begins to drift toward the poles.

At the poles, frigid, dense air sinks and leaves a "void" of missing air in the upper atmosphere. The warm air is drawn toward it.

We need to remember the Coriolis effect, though. As the warm air that's at high altitude, or at a high level above the ground, is moving toward the poles, it's curving to the east. In the tropics (near the equator), the Coriolis force is weak, so it's only a gentle eastward deflection.

Some of the air cools and sinks, descending to the surface and drying out the ground before returning to the equator. Meteorologists call this closed atmospheric circulation **the Hadley cell**. It's the reason why most parts of Africa and Australia away from the coastlines are barren deserts.

The rest of the warm air in the upper atmosphere continues moving toward the poles. It finds a stronger Coriolis force, which causes a more dramatic curve to its path. That shapes the air into swirling weather systems. Remember those? The highs and lows!

Meteorologists refer to this region as "the regime of eddy heat transport"—that's fancy-talk for "where a bunch of weather systems spin warm air toward the poles."

# HOW MUCH HEAT DOES THE ATMOSPHERE TRANSFER?

Weather systems are responsible for carrying heat around the world—specifically from warm areas to cold places. That means the heat doesn't move east to west, but rather north to south (and south to north). Thermal energy, a.k.a. heat, always travels from areas of higher temperature to areas of lower temperature.

But how much heat energy gets transferred? It turns out to be a *huge* number: up to 4 **petaWatts**. A Watt is a unit of power that measures the rate that energy is used or produced (specifically the rate that a source uses or produces one joule during one second). So if 1 petaWatt equals 1 *quadrillion* watts, that means that 4,000,000,000,000,000 Watts are being passed around!

That's a lot of power—about 217 times more energy than what all humans on Earth use combined!

↑ A low pressure system over the Gulf of Alaska on May 28, 2003, transports heat and moisture to the Arctic. (NASA)

# STORM SYSTEMS AND THE JET STREAM

Lows at the mid-latitudes, the areas of the earth that are between 30 and 60 degrees north and south of the equator, may be thousands of miles (kilometers) wide.

Low pressure systems generally move west to east. Because they're spinning, they draw in air masses from all sides. Warm, humid air is dragged poleward ahead of the storm. Cool, dry air crashes equatorward behind it.

The boundaries in between air masses are called **fronts**. Some fronts can be strong and sharp, with big spikes or drops in temperature over a short distance. Others may be barely noticeable, with very gradual temperature changes.

Warm fronts are often a bit more genteel. They bring fog, light precipitation, and thick clouds. Cold fronts can deliver more significant weather—heavy downpours, damaging winds, severe thunderstorms, or sudden bursts of snow (depending on the season).

↑ A low pressure system in the Gulf of Alaska on August 17, 2004. (NASA/MODIS)

## HOW STRONG DO FRONTS GET?

Some fronts can be extremely strong. On January 20, 1943, a front stalled in the Black Hills of South Dakota. It was bitterly cold to the north and cool to the south. As the stationary front wobbled back and forth, pockets of cold and warm air moved back and forth in the valleys, leading to erratic, and extreme, temperature changes.

In Spearfish, South Dakota, the temperature jumped from -4°F (-20°C) at 7:32 a.m. to 45°F (7°C) at 7:34 a.m. That's a 49°F (27°C) degree jump in just 2 minutes! Later that morning, it warmed to 54°F (12°C) degrees and then plunged back to -4°F (-20°C) within 27 minutes.

The temperature changes were so dramatic that peoples' windshields constantly frosted over as they drove between air pockets. Glass windows cracked.

↑ A temperature trace from Spearfish, South Dakota, during the erratic temperature swings of January 1943. The needle would move outward when temperatures were warmer. (U.S. National Weather Service)

polar jet stream

subtropical jet stream

## WHAT'S THE JET STREAM?

The **jet stream** is a band of strong winds several miles (kilometers) above the ground. Winds in the jet stream can exceed 200 miles per hour (mph), or 322 kilometers per hour (kph)—even if the air at the surface is perfectly still.

The jet stream forms due to temperature contrasts, or differences, between the equator and the poles. At the equator, air is warm, so the atmosphere expands vertically. At the North and South Poles, cold, dense air hugs the ground, and the height of the atmosphere shrinks. That means air in the upper atmosphere can "slide" down invisible slopes in the atmosphere.

Because of Earth's spin, however, that air curves east—so the "sliding" air can never actually reach the poles. Instead, it forms a highway of sorts. It circulates around the poles. The northern and southern hemispheres each have their own jet stream.

## AN AIRPLANE HIGHWAY

The jet stream plays a big role in air travel. That's because air traffic controllers, who instruct pilots where to fly, often plan routes based on where the jet stream is positioned. If a plane is flying east, it can get an extra boost in speed from the jet stream. It's like walking on a conveyor belt or moving walkway—even if you're walking the same speed, you're traveling faster because your surroundings are moving too!

The opposite thing can happen when planes are flying west. It usually takes them longer to reach their destination. Flight planners know this and budget extra time. That's why an average flight from New York to London take about 6 hours 50 minutes—but the return flight averages 8 hours 20 minutes!

On February 9, 2020, a British Airways Boeing 747 airplane flying between New York and London hit speeds of 825 mph (1,328 kph). That's 260 mph (418 kph) faster than normal! It completed the flight in a record 4 hours 56 minutes (almost two hours faster than usual). What was the reason? It was flying in a strong jet stream.

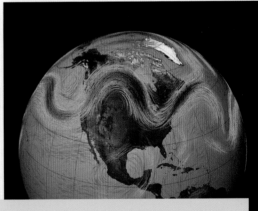

↑ A map of jet stream winds. (NASA)

# PRECIPITATION

Storm systems bring *precipitation*. Precipitation means any water that falls from the sky, such as rain, hail, snow, and sleet.

Precipitation forms when a pocket of humid air cools and can no longer hold its moisture. The extra moisture falls out of the cloud, plummeting to the ground.

Let's learn about the different types of precipitation:

**Rain** is the *liquid* form of water. Contrary to popular belief, raindrops are not tear-shaped. They are flat on the bottom and rounded at the top, like hamburger buns. That's because they encounter **air resistance**—when they fall, the air they're falling *through* pushes back on them.

**Snow** is the *frozen* form of water. Snowflakes begin as individual ice crystals that grow in a cloud. They begin when water droplets freeze onto a tiny piece of dust or pollen floating around in the air. Then, those ice crystals join other ice crystals.

**Sleet, graupel, and freezing rain** are all different forms of wintry precipitation. We'll learn more about that in our exciting chapter on winter storms. For now, just remember they all happen when air temperatures are close to freezing.

**Hail** is the most damaging form of precipitation. Individual **hailstones**, or chunks of ice, can grow to the size of bowling balls! They accompany severe thunderstorms. Hail forms because tall storm clouds carry water into the upper atmosphere.

## WETTEST AND DRIEST PLACES

The *wettest* place on Earth is Mawsynram, India. It's located in Meghalaya state in Northeastern India. Mawsynram averages 467.35 inches (11.87 m) of rain per year. More than 1,000 inches (2.54 m) fell in 1985! This spot gets so much rain because during the late summer, moisture from the Bay of Bengal moves north. It pools against the Himalayan Mountains, causing extreme precipitation.

↑ A vicuña in the Atacama Desert of Chile in 2021. (Matthew Cappucci)

The *driest* place on Earth is the Atacama Desert of Argentina and Chile. Parts of the desert are located between two mountain chains, the Chilean Coastal Range to the west and the Andes to the east, which block moisture from both directions.

# FLOODING

Flooding happens when too much rain falls. The ground can't absorb all the water, so the rest accumulates. Flooding is deadlier than tornadoes, hurricanes, and wildfires. Never drive through flooded roadways.

Flooding can happen any time it's raining, especially in cities—water falling on pavement and cement can't drain into the ground. But there are some weather situations that lead to a bigger risk of flooding.

**Tropical systems** and hurricanes can dump prolific rainfall totals—sometimes more than 3 feet (0.9 m)! That leads to major flooding.

↑ Flooding in Nashville, Tennessee, on May 4, 2010. (David Fine/FEMA)

**Atmospheric rivers** are narrow strips of rich tropical moisture that get tugged to the mid-latitudes. That can lead to significant rain or heavy snow—especially over mountainous regions. That's because atmospheric rivers carry most of their moisture a mile (1.6 km) above the ground. Mountains poke into that moisture and boost precipitation rates.

The word **monsoon** just means a seasonal wind shift. In some parts of the world, winds switch direction in the summertime. Instead of being dry, the winds draw in moisture from a body of water. That can lead to months of downpours and thunderstorms. Some places see 50 to 90 percent of their annual precipitation from only a few months of the monsoon season.

**Training** is the term given to downpours that move repeatedly over the same area. That happens if storms are riding a parked **boundary**, or front, like train cars on a train track.

↑ A dust storm approaching Spearman, Texas, on April 14, 1935. (NOAA collections)

# DROUGHT

Drought happens when a location doesn't receive *enough* rainfall compared to average. Some droughts last a few weeks. Others can persist for years or even decades.

Areas in drought often face resource shortages. Limited groundwater may affect farming. Food might become scarce, animals might shift from their natural habitats, and people sometimes have to relocate. Even shipping can become difficult if rivers run dry and ships can no longer navigate them.

In the 1930s, poor farming practices and drought over the central United States combined to produce the infamous Dust Bowl. Topsoil dried out, turned to dust, and blew away. Hardest hit were the Great Plains, but enormous choking dust clouds reached Chicago, New York City, and Boston.

# MAKE A CLOUD IN A BOTTLE

In this experiment, we'll understand the importance of *condensation nuclei*, learn about the role of temperature in forming cloud droplets, and make our very own cloud!

## THE SCIENCE BEHIND THE FUN:

This is how the atmosphere works! Sunshine heats water and it evaporates into a gas. Then, it floats into the sky, where it cools down and **condenses**, or turns into a liquid. That makes cloud droplets, and precipitation that falls to Earth, where it collects into ponds, lakes, rivers, and the ocean. Then, the process starts again! This is called **the water cycle**.

## HERE'S WHAT YOU'LL NEED:

+ Glass jar or soda bottle
+ Warm/hot tap water
+ Metal tray or tin
+ Ice
+ Spoon/stirrer
+ Match
+ An adult

1. Fill the jar with 2 inches (5 cm) of hot water. Some of the hot water will turn into an invisible gas called **water vapor**. You won't be able to see it.

2. Ask an adult to light a match. Then, blow it out and quickly drop the smoking match into the jar.

3. Put the lid on the jar. It will fill with smoke particles. These will act as **condensation nuclei**, or small itty-bitty pieces of material for water vapor to attach to when it cools down.

4. Place the covered jar in a tray of ice water. What happens? The jar and the water vapor gas inside are cooled down. Suddenly, a cloud appears! The water vapor has cooled from a gas to a liquid and landed on the little smoke particles.

5. Now, let's make the cloud disappear! Remove the jar from the tray of cool water. The temperature is warming, and the liquid water is evaporating or turning into an invisible gas, once again.

A thunderstorm towers over western Oklahoma on May 18, 2019.

## CHAPTER 3

# SEVERE THUNDERSTORMS

Some of the most wild—and scary—weather comes in the form of thunderstorms. Sometimes, thunderstorms are nice, like when we fall asleep to the sound of light rain on the rooftop and the occasional grumbles of thunder. Other times, thunderstorms can be destructive—slinging baseball-sized hail out of the sky at speeds topping 100 mph (161 kph) or delivering hurricane-force winds and tornadoes.

Thunderstorms can tower 10 or more miles (16 km) into the sky. They can rage for hours on end, traveling hundreds of miles (kilometers) and lasting for a day or more. Bolts of lightning frequently leap far from their cores, posing the danger of electrocution, and some thunderstorms even produce tornadoes.

In this chapter, we'll learn what makes a basic thunderstorm. We'll also talk about the different types of thunderstorms: clusters, squall lines, and the most dangerous of all, the supercell. We'll hear some storm stories about the most powerful thunderstorms on Earth. And, most importantly, we'll learn how to stay safe during severe weather.

# WHAT IS A THUNDERSTORM?

**M**ost thunderstorms form when different air masses meet. The resulting clash can brew instability.

Convection is a process that balances heat in the atmosphere. That's why air moves—and what drives weather systems and storms.

There are three main types of heat transfer in the atmosphere.

**Conduction** is the transfer of heat from objects that are in contact with one another. Imagine touching a pot of boiling water on the stove—*OUCH!* That's because heat is flowing directly into your hand since it's *touching* the heat source.

**Radiation** is heat transfer that occurs by waves moving through space. That's how sunlight works! The sun heats us up from 93 million miles (150 million km) away.

**Convection** describes heat transfer within a fluid. Fluids can be gases or liquids—any substance that doesn't have a given shape, like the ocean, or the atmosphere, or even a bowl of soup. Thunderstorms are examples of convection in the atmosphere. They occur when the atmosphere becomes **unstable**, meaning pockets of air near the ground are prone to rise because the air in the upper atmosphere is too cold and the air near the surface is too warm. Thunderstorms work to vertically balance heat.

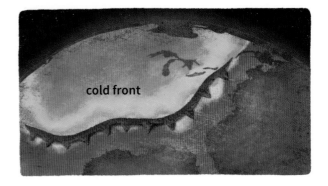

cold front

↑ Thunderstorms form along a cold front in Oklahoma on May 20, 2013.

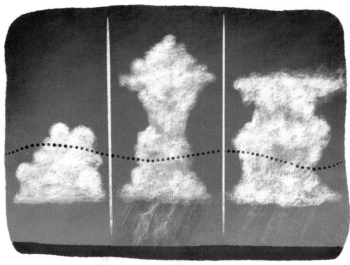

freezing level

developing stage

mature stage

dissipating stage

# THE UPDRAFT

Every thunderstorm has an **updraft** and a **downdraft**.

As air warms, it expands. That makes every unit of air *lighter* than the surrounding air. It's the same reason why hot air balloons float—the heated air swells, becoming less dense than the cooler air all around it, which lifts the balloon off the ground.

Updrafts carry warm, moist air high into the sky. They're like invisible chimneys. Water vapor, or invisible water gas, cools and condenses into cloud droplets. That conversion releases even more heat, known as **latent heat**, that warms the surrounding air and causes it to rise. That's why thunderstorms look like puffy heads of cauliflower—their billows mark plumes of upward-moving air. The most potent thunderstorms can have updrafts rushing upward at speeds of 100 mph (161 kph) or more.

Most updrafts stop when they reach the **tropopause**, or the "ceiling" of the troposphere, which is the lowest part of the atmosphere. Above the tropopause, air temperatures *warm* with height. That means the air in the thunderstorm updraft is no longer warmer than the surrounding air, and it stops rising. Oftentimes, the updraft goes *splat* against the tropopause and compresses into an **anvil cloud**, aptly named for its flat, anvil-shaped form. Thunderstorm anvils can spread miles (kilometers) outward in every direction. They're wispy and made out of ice crystals.

↑ A wintertime thunderstorm unleashes fierce bolts of electricity over Cape Cod Bay on February 21, 2014. Snow can be seen melting on the ground on the bottom left of the image. (Matthew Cappucci)

# THE DOWNDRAFT

Eventually, all the air that rises into a thunderstorm cools. That's because the updraft has carried it into the upper atmosphere, where air temperatures are well below freezing. The air is now also filled with rain and hail. That cools air pockets even more, making them heavier—and more dense—than the surrounding air.

That causes the air pockets to descend—sometimes very quickly. This is called the downdraft. Cool air rushes towards the ground and fans out in all directions. Sometimes, that causes strong winds. It's also accompanied by a cold rain and frequently, hail.

# THUNDER AND LIGHTNING

## WHAT MAKES LIGHTNING?

Lightning is a big spark. It can leap from the cloud to the ground, from the ground to the cloud, or between clouds.

Lightning forms due to **charges**, or the buildup of electricity. A unit of electricity is called an **electron**. Electrons are smaller than atoms and are too small to see even with microscopes. But if a lot of electrons move all at once, we see a glowing channel of electricity—lightning.

The purpose of lightning is to balance unequal charges. Perhaps a cloud has too *much* charge, and the ground doesn't have enough. Maybe it's the other way around. Lightning is just a river of electrons, or units of charge, jumping between the two. That helps them to balance. *Too many* electrons means a negative charge. If something is *missing* electrons, it has a positive charge. If the buildup of the opposite charges gets too big, *ZAP!* A bolt of lightning leaps through the air.

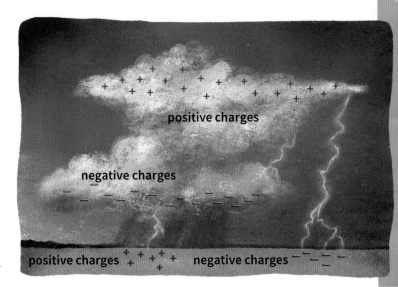

positive charges

negative charges

positive charges

negative charges

## WHAT IS THUNDER?

Lightning is five times hotter than the surface of the sun. It heats the air to 55,000°F (30,538°C). That causes the air to expand, creating an atmospheric shock wave. We hear that shock wave as thunder.

Thunder travels at the speed of sound, or 1,125 feet (343 m) per second. If you see a flash of lightning, you can count until you hear the thunder to estimate how far away it is. Every 5 seconds between the two represents 1 mile (1.6 km) of distance.

When lightning hits the ground, the electric charge can travel through whatever it strikes. The channel of electricity is even hot enough to melt sand! That fuses it into a glass-like rock called a **fulgurite**—basically fossilized lightning! Most lightning bolts are only 1 inch (2.5 cm) thick, but look bigger due to their brightness.

## CAN LIGHTNING STRIKE TWICE?

Yes! The Empire State Building in New York City was once struck 8 times in 24 minutes!

## WHAT'S THE LIGHTNING CAPITAL OF THE WORLD?

The lightning capital of the world is found in Venezuela—specifically, Lake Maracaibo, at the mouth of the Catatumbo River. An average of 603 lightning strikes hit every square mile of land per year! (That's 233 lightning strikes per square kilometer per year.) That number is based on 16 years' worth of data.

Lake Maracaibo

What's behind the extreme lightning barrages? Lake Maracaibo is home to the "everlasting thunderstorm." The lake sees thunderstorms an average of 297 nights per year. That's because it's perfectly shaped to produce strong thunderstorms almost every night.

As night falls, the ground cools off. The waters of the lake stay warm, however. That causes air to rise into powerhouse thunderstorms. They produce an exceptional amount of lightning!

In the United States, Oklahoma and Florida are the lightning capitals. Florida sees thunderstorms almost every day in the summertime. In 2022, Four Corners, a small town just west of Disney World, recorded, 1,229 lightning strikes per square mile (474 lightning strikes per square kilometer)!

# TYPES OF THUNDERSTORMS

**N**ot all thunderstorms are created equal. Most are weak and don't last very long. Others form in more volatile environments.

↑ A rotating thunderstorm near Atwood, Kansas, on May 26, 2021.

**Pulse-type thunderstorms** are the most common. They occur frequently in the summertime when winds in the upper atmosphere are weak. They move slowly—sometimes not at all. And they seldom last more than an hour. That's because they "rain themselves out." In other words, cool air falling in the downdraft interrupts, or chokes out, the updraft. That prevents warm, moist air from continuing to fuel the storm. Without energy sustaining it, the storm dies. That's why most pulse-type thunderstorms aren't very strong.

**Squall lines** are bands of thunderstorms that form along a boundary, such as a cold front, and stretch out along it. Some squall lines can be hundreds of miles (kilometers) from one end to another. They can survive for hours or even a day or more. Areas the size of several states can be hit by the same squall line if the storms are riding ahead of a cold front. **Derechos** are an especially intense type of squall line that live a long time, cover a lot of ground, and bring winds as strong as a hurricane.

**Supercells** are the strongest of all thunderstorms. That's because they spin. They form in environments where **wind shear** is present. Wind shear is a change of wind speed and/or direction with height. Because thunderstorms are so tall, they span multiple layers of atmosphere. If there is wind shear, a single thunderstorm will be pushed or pulled in many different directions. That causes the thunderstorm to rotate. Supercells are responsible for producing the strongest tornadoes. They also can produce giant hail.

## DID YOU KNOW?

Megaflashes are giant channels of lightning that can reach hundreds of miles (kilometers) long. They need a *big* storm to crawl through—like a squall line. This megaflash was 447 miles long!

↑ The GOES East weather satellite detected the megaflash on April 29, 2020. (NOAA/NWS)

## LIGHTNING SAFETY

The safest thing to do during a thunderstorm is to be indoors. Don't use metal plumbing or devices with wires. Lightning can travel through pipes or wires and electrocute you!

If you are caught outside and can't get to a building, crouch low to the ground and cover your head. Don't lie down though—only your feet should be touching the ground. Never seek shelter under a tree because the charge from a lightning strike can travel through the trunk and branches.

If your hair begins to stand on end or your mouth tastes strange, it may be a sign that lightning is about to strike! A charge is building up on you. Evacuate the area immediately. Always remember that you *never* want to be the tallest object in an area.

In the United States, lightning kills an average of 20 people per year. Hundreds of others are injured. About 80 percent of lightning strike victims survive, but some have permanent disabilities after.

If you encounter a lightning strike victim, immediately call 911 (or your emergency telephone number, if different) to get professional medical attention. The electricity from lightning commonly disrupts the electrical impulses responsible for making your heart beat, causing cardiac arrest. If the victim is unresponsive and not breathing, anyone who is CPR certified (trained in cardiopulmonary resuscitation) can begin administering mouth-to-mouth and chest compressions.

↑ A lightning strike in Nebraska in 2022.

# THUNDERSTORM HAZARDS

**N**ow that we understand what makes a thunderstorm and how thunderstorms organize, let's learn about their hazards.

## HAIL

Hail is a type of ice that forms in thunderstorms. Hail forms when a thunderstorm updraft carries liquid water high in the sky. The biggest thunderstorms might be 12 miles (19 km) or more tall. That's *twice* the altitude at which you might fly in a commercial airplane!

If you've ever felt the window when on a flight, you probably noticed how cold it was. It's *always* cold in the upper atmosphere—even on summer days when it's hot at ground level.

When raindrops get carried into the cold areas of the atmosphere, they freeze. That makes pellets of ice. Supercooled water droplets, which are droplets of water that remain in liquid form at subfreezing temperatures, coat the tiny ice pebble—freezing onto it and causing it to grow.

Eventually, the hail falls to the ground. Sometimes, it melts before reaching the surface, turning back into rain. Other times, chunks of ice hit the ground.

The largest hailstones can reach the size of baseballs or bigger! A hailstone will continue to grow in a cloud so long as an updraft can hold it in midair. Once the hailstone gets too heavy, it falls.

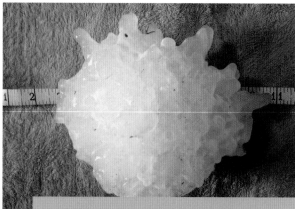

↑ This Vivian, South Dakota, hailstone is the largest on record. (NWS Aberdeen)

### DID YOU KNOW?

If you look at a smashed-up hailstone, it will resemble an onion with visible layers inside. Some layers of ice are clear. That's because the water froze more slowly and air bubbles escaped. Other layers are white and opaque, meaning that the ice formed quickly.

# THE BIGGEST HAILSTONE EVER RECORDED

It takes hailstones the size of a golf ball to dent vehicles or break glass. But hailstones can be *much* bigger. Scientists invented a name for the most massive hailstones—those that reach 6 inches (15 cm) or more across. They're called **gargantuan** hail. They're rare, but they're disastrous.

The biggest hailstone ever directly measured fell on Vivian, South Dakota, on July 23, 2010. A very strong supercell thunderstorm produced winds up to 85 mph (137 kph), with a couple of brief tornadoes nearby. Temperatures were in the 90s°F (30s°C) at the surface, but were around -96°F (-71°C) degrees at the top of the storm. That meant *extreme* instability and extreme updrafts capable of massive hail.

Once the storm was over, Les Scott, a resident of Vivian, collected one of the stones. It was 8 inches (20 cm) in diameter and weighed 1.94 pounds (879.97 g). That's bigger than a volleyball!

A meteorologist from the National Weather Service office in Aberdeen, South Dakota, was sent to measure the stone and certify it as a record. By the time they got there, it had likely melted a bit and shrunk, and it was *still* a record! Hail the size of corn cobs fell on Carlos Paz in Córdoba, Argentina on February 8, 2018. They were between 7.4 and 9.3 inches (18.8 and 23.6 cm)across!

↑ A crater in the ground left by the hailstone. (NWS Aberdeen)

↑ Hail blasted through this deck in Vivian. (NWS Aberdeen)

↑ Meteorologists measure the circumference of the stone. (NWS Aberdeen)

# MICROBURSTS

**M**icrobursts are a type of very localized downburst. They can be extremely small but intense.

Scientists didn't know about microbursts until the 1970s because they are so small in scale. However, the crash of Eastern Airlines Flight 66 on June 24, 1975, captured the attention of meteorologists. While landing at John F. Kennedy Airport in New York City during a thunderstorm, the plane was pushed downward by strong winds. The aircraft crashed, killing 113 people onboard.

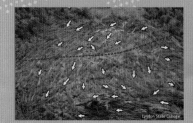

↑ Tornadoes (left) pull objects toward the center of their path in a swirling pattern. Microbursts (right) are winds that fan debris outward. (NWS/Lyndon State College)

A renowned Japanese scientist named Dr. Ted Fujita later developed a theory about what had happened. He believed a narrow lobe of downward-moving air rushed toward the ground within the storm. That reduced lift, causing the plane to lose altitude and crash. Over the next ten years, he researched other events. He eventually concluded that strong thunderstorms could produce **microbursts**, or extremely strong, tiny downbursts.

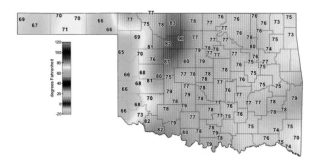

↑ A temperature map from sunrise on May 11, 2022, when a heat burst spiked the temperature from 68°F (20°C) in Lahoma, Oklahoma, to 90°F (32°C). (Oklahoma Mesonet)

## HEAT BURSTS

Heat bursts are a rare form of dry microburst that brings a hot, dry wind. They usually occur at night with decaying thunderstorms. As the updraft of a thunderstorm dies, any leftover precipitation-cooled air rushes toward the ground. That air is squished as it approaches the ground, heating up and drying out.

On June 4, 2020, the temperature in Spencer, Oklahoma, jumped from 80°F (27°C) degrees at 9:05 p.m. to 97°F (36°C) at 10:10 p.m. beneath dissipating thunderstorms. A heat burst in 2012 in Stillwater, Oklahoma, spiked the temperature of 83°F (28°C) at 12:25 a.m. to 95°F (35°C) just 10 minutes later. And on May 14, 2020, a morning heat burst in Chandler, Oklahoma, helped temperatures climb from the 60s to 81°F, with 65 mph (105 kph) winds. During each episode, humidities plummeted as the air rapidly dried out.

Until the later 1900s, heat bursts were poorly understood. People sometimes even sprinted out of their homes during heat bursts since they assumed their houses were on fire!

# THUNDERSTORMS

Earlier in the chapter, we learned that the sound of thunder takes about 5 seconds to travel 1 mile (1.6 km). Next time you experience a thunderstorm, try it—while you're safely inside, of course.

1. When you see the first flash of lightning, begin counting—one one thousand, two one thousand, three one thousand . . . and so on, until you hear *BOOM!*

2. Look for patterns. Does the thunder sound like a sharp clap, or does it crackle and rumble for a long period of time? Why do you think that is? (Hint: Think about the shape of a lightning bolt and where the sound of thunder is coming from. Does thunder come only from where lightning hits the ground? Or does it emanate from the whole lightning channel?)

3. Pay attention to the last rumble of thunder you hear. Then, wait *another* 30 minutes before going outside. Why? Because lightning can leap 10 miles (16 km) or more from a thunderstorm! Positive bolts, which shoot out the top of thunderclouds, can travel far distances. Even if it's sunny outside, you can still be struck by lightning.

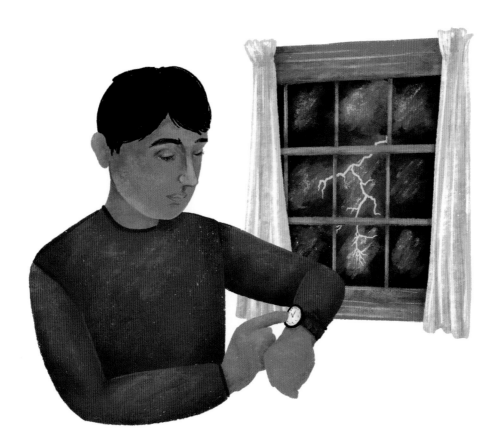

A tornado near Lockett, Texas, on April 23, 2021.

## CHAPTER 4

# TORNADOES

Tornadoes are the most violent type of windstorms on Earth. They are narrow funnels of wind that are connected to the base of a tall cloud, like a downpour or a thunderstorm. Most tornadoes are weak and only last a few minutes—but the strongest can last hours and have winds up to 300 mph (483 kph).

Tornadoes come with little warning. Meteorologists try to alert residents before a tornado happens, but knowing where—and when—a tornado will strike is difficult. Most people only have a few seconds or minutes of notice and have to act quickly to hide from the windstorm.

In this chapter, we'll discuss what tornadoes are. We'll understand what makes a tornado, and we'll learn how we can stay safe.

## DID YOU KNOW?

A tornado watch means conditions are favorable for the development of severe weather, including tornadoes. It basically means to "watch out."

A warning is issued on a much smaller scale, usually for only a couple of towns. A warning means that a tornado is believed to be forming or occurring. Either a tornado has been spotted, or meteorologists detect rotation on radar.

# WHAT IS A TORNADO?

Tornadoes are columns of wind. Most hang underneath a thunderstorm. They form from rotation inside the storm clouds. If a tube of that rotation touches the ground, a tornado is born.

Tornadoes come in all shapes and sizes. Some are only a few feet (1 m) wide. Others can swallow entire towns. They can happen at any time of the day or night. Some tornadoes are cloaked in rain and impossible to see.

The majority of tornadoes look like elephant trunks, funnels, or trumpets. They poke out of dark, angry clouds.

Some people call tornadoes **twisters**. Other people refer to them as **cyclones** or **whirlwinds**. No matter what they're called, they're dangerous. If you see a tornado, you should get to a safe place right away. The winds of a tornado can be damaging or even deadly.

## HOW DOES A TORNADO FORM?

Tornadoes develop in the updraft region of the storm. That's where warm, moist air spirals inward and upward. As the updraft moves faster, a more concentrated area of rotation might start to form.

Eventually, a column of spin 2 to 5 miles (3 to 8 km) across forms within the storm. Meteorologists call this the **mesocyclone**. From the bottom of the mesocyclone, a rugged, churning, cylinder-shaped cloud begins reaching toward the ground. This is the **wall cloud**.

Usually a plume of cool, dense air descends to the ground behind the wall cloud. That wraps around the circulation, tightening it, and can make wall cloud spin faster. Sometimes, a funnel cloud will form— a pointed cloud that looks like an elephant's trunk. If the spinning winds touch the ground, it's a tornado.

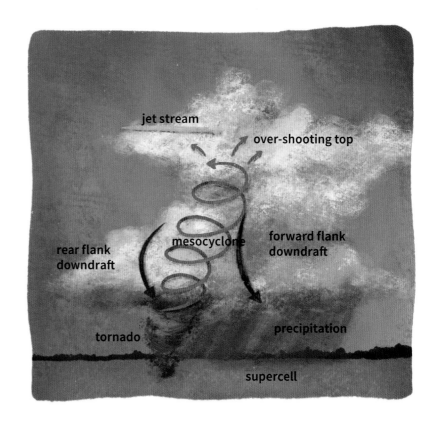

jet stream

over-shooting top

forward flank downdraft

rear flank downdraft

mesocyclone

tornado

precipitation

supercell

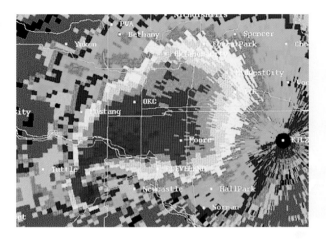

← Radar can't "see" air, but can see what's in the air. That means rain or hail! When strong rotation is present in a storm, the winds swirl rain and hail around that column of spin. That creates a hook, marking where the rotation is. Meteorologists call this telltale signal a "hook echo." A hook (bottom left) appears on radar as rain and hail are swirled around an F5 tornado. The tornado hit Moore, Oklahoma, killing 36 people on May 3, 1999.

↑ A rotating thunderstorm over Dibble, Oklahoma, approaching the town of Cole, on May 11, 2023.

↑ A wall cloud appears from the base of the storm.

↑ A funnel cloud drops from the wall cloud.

↑ The tornado touches down.

# TYPES OF SUPERCELLS

Most tornadoes come from supercell thunderstorms. But there are different types of supercells, and they can affect what a tornado looks like and if you can see it. The three main types of supercell thunderstorms:

**Classic supercells** have a wet region of the storm—the downdraft—and a mostly rain-free updraft. Heavy rain and hail falls in the downdraft. Since the updraft is rain-free, the tornado is usually visible.

→ A classic supercell on May 17, 2021, near Forsan, Texas. Notice the tornado protruding from the updraft. Softball-sized hail is falling in the downdraft, which appears dark, to the right.

**HP, or high precipitation, supercells** have a *ton* of water. Rain and hail swirl around the tornado, hiding it from view. That makes HP supercells *especially* dangerous. It's why you should *never* wait to see or hear a tornado before taking shelter—sometimes you can't!

← A high precipitation supercell west of Kansas City on May 28, 2019. At the time, a powerful EF4 tornado was on the ground, hidden in the rain.

**LP, or low precipitation, supercells** are mostly rain-free. They fling out large hailstones though, so don't underestimate their dangers! They also crackle with plenty of thunder and lightning, but don't usually produce tornadoes.

→ A low precipitation supercell near Atwood, Kansas, on May 26, 2021.

# TORNADO FAST FACTS

**BIGGEST:**
May 31, 2013, El Reno, Oklahoma.
**2.6 miles (4.2 km) wide.**

**FASTEST WINDS:**
May 3, 1999, Moore, Oklahoma.
**301 mph (484 kph).**

**LONGEST TRACK:**
March 18, 1925, Missouri, Illinois, and Indiana.
**219 miles (352 km).** (It may have been multiple tornadoes with overlapping tracks.)

**DEADLIEST:**
April 26, 1989, Daulatpur–Saturia, Bangladesh.
**Killed approximately 1,300** people due to crowded neighborhoods and poor home construction.

**WORST TORNADO OUTBREAK:**
April 25 to 28, 2011.
A storm **system produced 360 tornadoes** across the United States and Canada. 324 people died.

↑ A tornado on the southern side of Lockett, Texas, on April 23, 2021.

## DID YOU KNOW?

Many tornadoes actually have smaller whirlwinds within them. These are called **multi-vortex tornadoes**. A single tornado might be made up of five or ten very narrow funnels orbiting a common center. That makes for strips of intense—and erratic—damage.

# STORM CHASE ADVENTURES

## THE ANNAPOLIS, MARYLAND, TORNADO

Meteorologists had been worried for days about a possible tornado outbreak on Wednesday, September 1, 2021—including me. The leftovers of Hurricane Ida were moving up the United States Eastern Seaboard. Ida was a strong Category 4 hurricane that hit Louisiana with winds gusting as high as 172 mph (277 kph).

Even though Ida had weakened and was no longer a hurricane, it was still dangerous. That's because the remnants of tropical systems are known for spawning tornadoes. And tornadoes in the Deep South tend to move more quickly.

Ida's leftovers were expected to arrive in the Mid-Atlantic and Northeast on Wednesday. As a TV meteorologist at WTTG Channel 5 in Washington, D.C., I had been warning viewers about the threat of tornadoes since the Sunday before.

## THE DAY OF THE STORM

When Wednesday rolled around, the atmosphere looked volatile. Morning sunshine had heated the lower atmosphere, causing it to become more unstable. That meant there would be more "juice" to fuel thunderstorms.

That afternoon, I decided to drive about 30 miles (48 km) east of Washington, D.C. That's where the atmosphere was a little bit more humid. I also noticed easterly winds at the surface, which would enhance low-level twist. The ingredients were in place for a tornado.

## KEY DETAILS

**Location:**
Annapolis, Maryland, USA

**Date:**
September 1, 2021

**Type of Storm:**
Tornado

↓ A photograph of the tornado I intercepted in Annapolis, Maryland, USA, on September 1, 2021.

## CHASING A TORNADO

As I raced east on the highway, I glanced at a dashboard-mounted radar display. I knew a rotating thunderstorm was located to my southeast. I accelerated toward the city of Annapolis.

Five minutes before I exited the highway, heavy rain engulfed my vehicle. I could barely see 30 feet (9 m) in front of me. As the flooding rains poured down, a loud, shrill *EEEEEEEEEEK* from my phone startled me. It was an emergency alert. We were under a tornado warning.

I glanced to the south at the storm clouds now gathering. The entire sky was jet black. I saw an angry cloud that formed a backwards C shape that tightened to a point in the distance. Beneath that point was a triangle-like cloud that reminded me of an elephant trunk sniffing the ground. Could it be? It *was* a tornado—in Maryland! And I was only 3 miles (5 km) away!

I drove to a parking lot and climbed onto the roof of my truck for a better look—but could barely see the cylinder-shaped cloud mass churning above the tree line. I decided to race northward once again. After about 5 minutes, I was face to face with the tornado.

## INTERCEPT

It was only 800 feet (244 m) to my northwest as I crossed Weems Creek, a small river just off the Chesapeake Bay. To my right, sailboats floated lazily, the water glass-calm. To my left, an angry, vaporous mass of smoke was snatching tree limbs into the air.

A confetti of debris was swirling around the furious tornado, but shafts of sunlight were poking through gaps in the cloud cover. Individual shreds of debris twinkled as they slipped through each channel of light. They shimmered like sparkles in an otherwise sinister storm.

After a few moments, a burst of cold, heavy rainfall arrived, as if the world's biggest lawn sprinkler had suddenly decided to turn on. This was the **rear flank downdraft**, or wraparound of rain-chilled, dense air on the back side of the tornadic circulation.

## IDA'S HISTORIC FLOODING

I spent the next 9 hours on TV, breaking down what had happened. The tornado was rated an EF2 with 125 mph (201 kph) winds. It ripped the roofs off people's homes and completely demolished some structures.

Later that night, the same tropical remnants moved into New Jersey and New York, bringing historic flooding as moisture pooled along an approaching cold front. That meant incredible rainfall rates—Newark International Airport also recorded their wettest day on record with 8.41 inches (21.36 cm) falling by midnight. A total of 53 people died in the flooding.

# WHERE DO TORNADOES HAPPEN?

The United States is the tornado capital of the world. More than 1,200 of them happen each year.

Some happen across the border in Canada too. North America is home to the perfect combination of ingredients for tornadoes. Warm, moist air from the Gulf of Mexico clashes with chilly Canadian air sliding down the Rockies. That makes for big thunderstorms. The jet stream overhead, meanwhile, helps thunderstorms rotate. During the springtime, especially March, April, May, and June, hundreds of tornadoes can touch down per month.

Tornadoes also occasionally happen in a few other parts of the world. Argentina and Uruguay, in South America, see a few each year. Europe gets tornadoes too, though many probably are missed and aren't counted. Many tornadoes in Europe happen in rural areas, and damage isn't always surveyed to determine if a tornado occurred. There also isn't one central

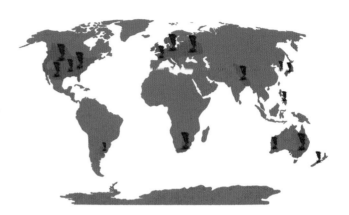

A map of where tornadoes occur around the world.

database of tornadoes like there is in the United States. That means record-keeping is incomplete. Parts of India, Bangladesh, eastern China, Australia, Japan, the Philippines, New Zealand, and South Africa also experience tornadoes.

## TORNADO COUNTRY

Many people talk about an area of the central United States called **Tornado Alley**. It's a corridor of Texas, Oklahoma, Kansas, Nebraska, Colorado, and the Dakotas where there are a lot of tornadoes. For decades, news organizations depicted Tornado Alley as if it was the number-one zone for tornadoes. But that's not exactly true.

The real bull's-eye for tornado risk in the United States is actually in Mississippi and Alabama. They see just as many tornadoes, if not more, than high-risk states like Oklahoma and Texas. According to research, what's the most dangerous place in the world for tornadoes? Smith County, Mississippi. So why is the Deep South of the United States so often forgotten?

For starters, most of Tornado Alley's twisters happen within a six-week window during late April and most of May.

## DID YOU KNOW?

People are more vulnerable to tornadoes in the Deep South than they are on the Great Plains. The tornadoes are often more powerful and faster-moving. More people live in mobile homes, and even a weak tornado can destroy a mobile home.

All things considered, it's important that people realize that Tornado Alley is an outdated concept. The real zone of tornado risk in the United States encompasses a much broader area. That's why having a tornado plan is important. Tornadoes can—and do—strike in any season.

But in the Deep South, tornadoes are more spread out over a seven-month window from November to June. That makes it easier to overlook how many actually touch down.

Tornadoes also *look* different in different places. Tornado Alley, located over the U.S. Great Plains, is in a part of the country where the land is flat. There aren't many trees. So tornadoes can be easily seen and photographed. Those are the ones that appear in newspapers, on TV, and in movies. The tornadoes are also taller and more likely to look like a classic funnel shape.

In the Deep South, more moisture means more rugged clouds around a tornado. That makes them difficult to see. And views are blocked by pine tree forests and rolling hills. Most of the tornadoes are invisible until it's too late. Since fewer pictures are taken, people underestimate tornado risk.

Tornadoes in the Deep South, especially around Tennessee, Mississippi, Alabama, and Georgia, are also more likely to occur at night. Between a third and half of tornadoes there spin up after dark.

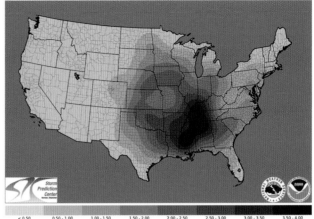

Mean Number of EF2+ Tornado Days per Decade Within 25 Miles of a Point 1986 - 2015

< 0.50   0.50 - 1.00   1.00 - 1.50   1.50 - 2.00   2.00 - 2.50   2.50 - 3.00   3.00 - 3.50   3.50 - 4.00

↑ A map of where significant tornadoes are common. Notice the greatest risk is in Mississippi, Alabama, and Tennessee. (NOAA/SPC)

# HOW ARE TORNADOES RATED?

It's usually impossible to directly measure the winds inside a tornado. That's why scientists and engineers have teamed up to build on work that Dr. Fujita conducted in the 1970s. By looking at the damage left by a tornado, meteorologists are now able to guess how strong it was. Tornadoes are rated on the Enhanced Fujita (EF) scale.

Most tornadoes, about 80 percent, are EF0 or EF1 in strength. That means winds are below 110 mph (177 kph). Only 1 percent of tornadoes are "violent"— EF4 or EF5 in strength. EF5 tornadoes have winds over 200 mph (322 kph). They strip the pavement off roadways, scour the ground bare, carve trenches into the dirt, and can toss trains like toys.

↑ The dent in this water tower was caused by an EF5 tornado on April 27, 2011, in Smithville, Mississippi. The tornado tossed a red Ford Explorer half a mile (0.8 km) into the water tower. (NOAA/University of Alabama Huntsville/ University Space Research Association)

# OTHER TYPES OF TORNADOES

Not all tornadoes form from rotation within clouds.

**Landspouts** are a weak type of tornado that begin with preexisting spin near the ground. That weak surface whirl moves beneath a towering cloud. Then, the cloud's updraft vertically stretches the spin. That can form an EF0 or EF1 tornado.

**Waterspouts** are tornadoes over water. Some form the same way as landspouts and generally have winds less than 50 mph (80 kph). These are sometimes referred to as **fair-weather waterspouts**. The Florida Keys record 100 waterspouts or more per month in the summertime.

**Snow tornadoes** sound impossible. They form like ordinary tornadoes, but when temperatures are below freezing. That means the air in the upper atmosphere has to be incredibly cold.

↑ A snow tornado hitting Andros Island, Greece, on January 24, 2022. Notice the snowflakes in the image. (Meteo.GR/WebcamGreece.com)

## FIRE TORNADOES

What could be scarier than a tornado? How about a tornado made out of *fire*?!

Fire tornadoes are different from fire whirls. **Fire whirls** are the tiny eddies of flame that form over campfires or brushfires. Fire tornadoes are actual tornadoes.

Generating a fire tornado requires an *enormous* amount of heat from a big fire. That heat and smoke billows high in the sky, sometimes to 9.5 miles (15 km). A plume that tall can act like a thundercloud. If the winds in the atmosphere change direction with height, that smoke plume can rotate. Sometimes, the smoke plume even spits out lightning strikes.

Then, it's like forming a regular tornado. Fire-heated air spiraling into the smoke plume rotates faster and faster. Then, a tornado can happen.

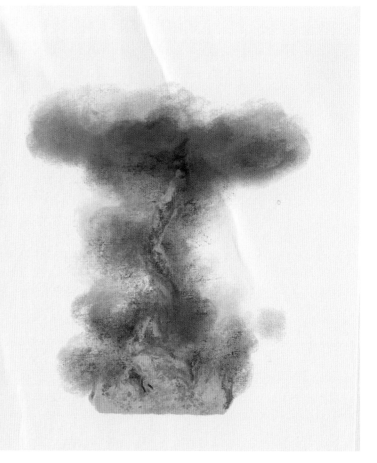

# TORNADO OUTBREAKS

When conditions are favorable for tornadoes, more than one can form at once. Sometimes, *many* happen on the same day. This is called a **tornado outbreak**.

A single supercell thunderstorm can produce several tornadoes. And, if a large-scale storm system is powerful enough, lots of supercell thunderstorms can be raging at the same time. The biggest outbreaks feature hundreds of tornadoes. On rare occasions, the same location can be hit twice in the same day.

In the right environments, supercell thunderstorms "cycle." That means they produce a tornado, it lifts, the storm reorganizes, and a new tornado forms. One storm that tore through central Oklahoma on May 3, 1999, produced 20 individual tornadoes!

↑ An aerial view of tornado damage in Tuscaloosa, Alabama, following the 2011 super outbreak. (NWS Birmingham)

⚠ Every 40 or 50 years, on average, a **super outbreak** occurs. On April 3, 1974, for example, 148 tornadoes spun up from Alabama to Ohio. The same zone was hit by an even worse outbreak from April 25 to 28, 2011. An unbelievable 360 tornadoes hit during that time, killing 348 people.

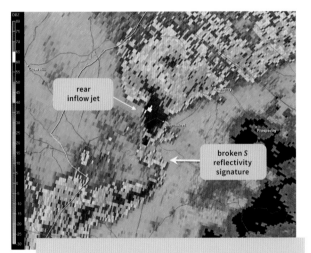

↑ A radar map of a tornadic circulation in an HSLC line of storms. Notice the line bends back and forms a kink where the tornado is developing. The tornado hit Newberry County, South Carolina, on February 28, 2011.

## HSLC TORNADOES

In addition to supercellular tornadoes, there are also HSLC tornadoes—which stands for "high-shear, low-CAPE." They're tornadoes that form when shear, or spin, is plentiful, but there's not much convective available potential energy (CAPE), or juice, to fuel thunderstorms.

During HSLC setups, winds change direction quickly with height. That causes areas of spin to form at the bottom of the squall line. Sometimes, mesocyclones are too shallow for radars to detect. That makes it difficult for meteorologists to issue advance tornado warnings before they are created.

# STORM CHASE ADVENTURES

On May 24, 2021, I woke up in Colby, a small town in northwest Kansas. The weather was gross — it was 58°F (14°C) outside, and a cool mist was falling. Skies were overcast. I knew that storms would be unlikely to form in such a cold environment.

When I scoured the Internet for weather data, however, I noticed something interesting: just a 20-minute drive to my south, it was sunny and warm. That would mean fuel for severe thunderstorms as a weather disturbance approached. There would be plenty of **vorticity**, or spin, to help storms spiral. The chase was on!

I drove 90 minutes south. Brilliant sunshine was heating the ground. Thunderstorms developed by 4 p.m. I chased a couple, but none produced tornadoes.

That's when I began hearing about reports of tornadoes *near Colby*, just north of my hotel! Wasn't it too cold for tornadoes? I found out that the northern edge of the warm air had moved north, spilling into the town. That pushed the warm front, or boundary between warm air south and cool air to the north, north of Colby. When thunderstorms form and anchor themselves to warm fronts, surprise tornadoes can spin up. That's because warm fronts have lots of low-level **helicity**, or potential for rotation. That feeds into storms and helps make tornadoes.

I drove back to Colby as quickly as I could. When I approached the town, I noticed a thunderhead, or thunderstorm, out my right window. It was still just an ordinary thunderstorm, but I had a feeling it was hiding something.

**Location:**
Selden, Kansas, USA

**Date:**
May 24, 2021

**Type of Storm:**
Tornado

↓ An ominous cone funnel appears from within the rain near Selden, Kansas, on May 24, 2021.

4:00
Monday, May 24

⚠ Emergency Alert

National Weather Services
TORNADO WARNING

I tapped my GPS to route me to the town of Selden, a 30-mile (48 km) drive from Colby. The thundercloud had a strange blue tint to it. As I drew nearer, my phone buzzed—*tornado warning*. Game on.

The road curved east. To my left, I noticed a plume of rain and hail dropping out of the storm just north of the roadway. That was the rear flank downdraft. If the storm had a tornado, it would be on the other side.

Suddenly, I squinted. "Is that a funnel?" I wondered. Through the veil of precipitation, I could barely discern a cone-shaped cloud. Thirty seconds later, I was sure. "It *is* a tornado!" I thought.

Five minutes later, I was barely a quarter mile (0.4 km) away from it. Multiple whirls danced around each other like wrestling snakes. The tornado crossed the road, damaging buildings in the town of Selden. I parked my truck on the edge of the highway and stepped outside to take pictures.

Out of nowhere, a blast of hot wind almost knocked me down. *Crunch!* It bent my open car door on its hinges, preventing me from closing it. I realized I was in the rear flank downdraft, but it was *warm*. That's highly unusual. It's likely that the strangely warm burst of air helped the tornado form in the first place.

↓ A collar of blue wraps around the funnel cloud that is emerging. The condensation funnel is beginning to materialize.

↑ The tornado crossing the road and destroying buildings.

# TORNADO IN A BOTTLE

**W**e can't *actually* make a tornado, but we can visualize how a whirlwind works!

## THE SCIENCE BEHIND THE FUN:

You'll see a funnel-shaped whirlpool appear in front of you. Notice what happens—after you stop shaking, the funnel eventually lifts back up, and the dip in the water flattens. That's how a tornado works! The inward vacuum-like tug of a tornado is the same. Once the vortex weakens, the spin slows down.

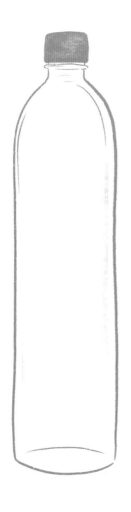

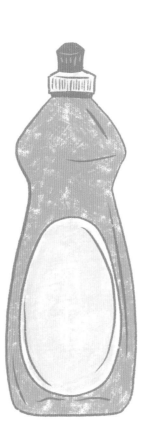

## HERE'S WHAT YOU'LL NEED:

+ **Clear plastic water bottle**
+ **Food coloring**
+ **Glitter**
+ **Dish soap**
+ **Water**

1.  Fill the water bottle three-quarters of the way to the top with water.

2.  Add a squirt of your favorite shade of food coloring. Then, sprinkle the glitter into the water.

3.  Add a drop of dish soap.

4.  Seal the container, making sure the lid or cap is on tight!

5.  Then, swirl it up, shaking it in circles!

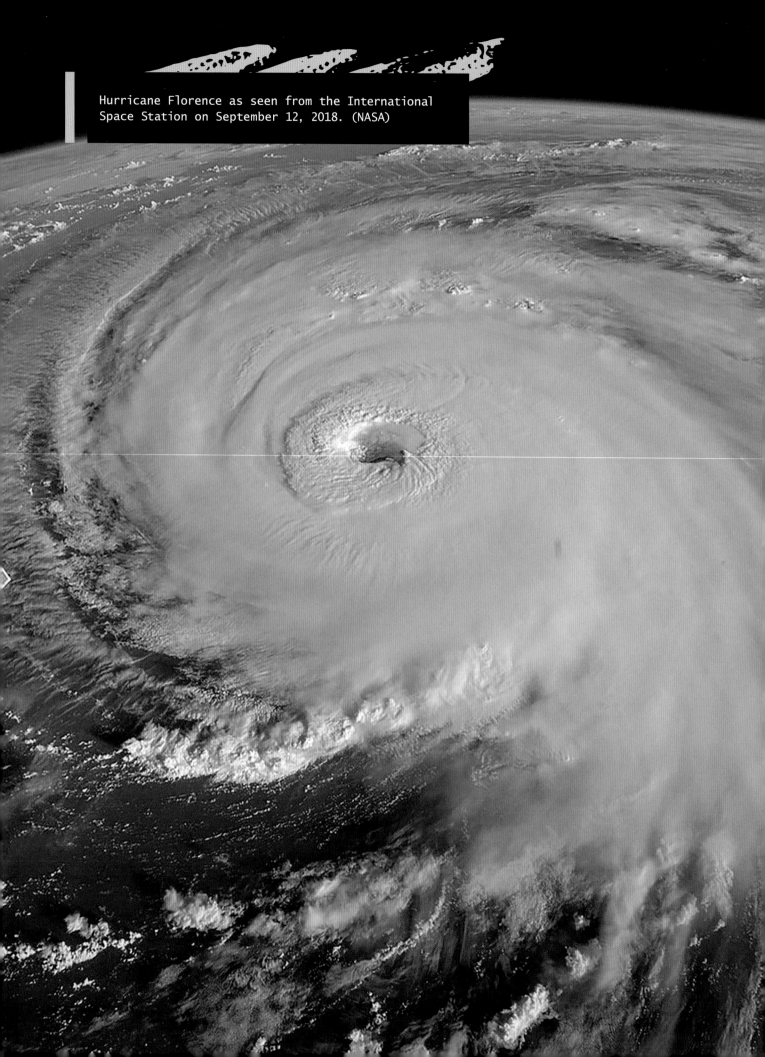

Hurricane Florence as seen from the International
Space Station on September 12, 2018. (NASA)

## CHAPTER 5:

# HURRICANES AND TROPICAL CYCLONES

Hurricanes are some of the biggest—and scariest—storms on planet Earth.
They can be up to 500 miles (805 km) wide, contain winds of 150 mph (241 kph),
and unleash flooding rains and tornadoes.

Hurricanes are a type of **tropical cyclone**, or a storm system that forms in the tropics, which are the regions on Earth where it's warm year-round. They feed off warm ocean waters. The hotter the waters, the stronger a hurricane can get.

Even though hurricanes *form* where the waters are warm, they can travel away from the tropics. Some have even made it as far away as Canada or even Brazil!

Hurricanes have different names around the world. Around the Atlantic Ocean, they're called **hurricanes**—but in the west Pacific, they're called **typhoons**. Australians call them **cyclones**, and in India, people refer to them as **cyclonic storms**.

No matter where they strike, hurricanes are a problem—especially for residents near the coast. Authorities frequently evacuate coastal communities before a hurricane's arrival. That's where the wind and coastal flooding is most extreme.

Heavy rain can cause freshwater flooding up to 1,000 miles (1,609 km) inland, too. Most tropical cyclone deaths come from inland flooding.

In this chapter, we'll learn all about hurricanes and tropical storms—what makes them, why they're dangerous, and how to stay safe. And we'll discuss how the warming world is changing hurricanes and what storms of the future might look like.

# BIRTH OF A HURRICANE

A hurricane begins as a broad, weak atmospheric disturbance known as a **tropical wave**. Think of a tropical wave as a seed that could later grow into a storm. There are hundreds of tropical waves that form around the world every year. Only about 90 turn into hurricanes, cyclones, or typhoons.

In the Atlantic, tropical waves roll off the coast of Africa every couple of days between late July and the end of September. Other tropical waves can materialize on their own in the Pacific and Indian oceans, or even around Australia.

↑ A tropical wave exiting Africa south of the Cabo Verde Islands on July 22, 2013. (NOAA)

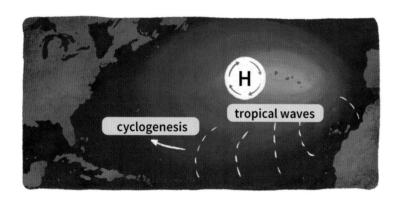

Tropical waves feature **convergence** near the sea surface. That means air gathers toward the same point. As pockets of gathering air collide, they force each other upward. That rising air makes a clumping of downpours and thunderstorms.

Since winds in the upper atmosphere over the tropics are weak, the thunderstorms are pulse-type storms. They tower high, but individual storms rain themselves out after an hour or so. That's because one cell's *downdraft* interrupts a neighboring cell's *updraft*. In other words, the thunderstorms choke each other. That can kill the tropical waves.

For the thunderstorms to survive, they have to work together. That means their updrafts and downdrafts can't interfere. The storms arrange themselves around a common center of low pressure. Individual thunderstorm cells breathe air inward from all around the thunderstorm cluster. The storms extract heat and moisture from the air, using that as fuel to grow stronger. Then, the storms exhale the processed air outward at high altitudes, pushing it away from the storm cluster.

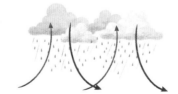

**Disorganized thunderstorms;** one storm chokes of other

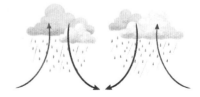

**Organized thunderstorms;** storms align downdrafts to not choke off updrafts

# AN ORGANIZING SYSTEM

As the thunderstorm cluster intensifies, it might grow large enough to feel the Earth's rotation. That will make it spin.

Strengthening thunderstorms lift more air away from the sea surface. That causes the low pressure in the middle of the thunderstorm cluster to intensify since there's now less air, and less weight, overhead. The stronger low pressure acts as a vacuum, pulling air in from all around. That strengthens the winds.

If a closed circulation, or area of spin, exists, the system might be declared a tropical depression. Tropical depressions have winds less than 38 mph (61 kph). Once winds hit 39 mph (63 kph), it's declared a tropical storm.

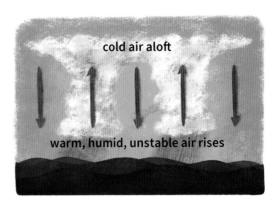

cold air aloft

warm, humid, unstable air rises

It's very rare for a tropical cyclone to form near the equator since the Coriolis force is weakest there.

# LOW RIDERS

Tropical cyclones derive their spin from the Coriolis force. Since the Coriolis force is zero on the equator, a hurricane can't happen there. In fact, it was once believed a hurricane couldn't form within 5 degrees latitude of the equator. Storms near the equator are called *low riders*.

Technically speaking, a well-developed hurricane could *cross* the equator. The powerful inward pull of the storm's strong, swirling low pressure would dominate over the weak Coriolis force. That means the storm could keep spinning.

But that's never happened. The reason? In addition to governing which way a storm spins, the Coriolis force also works to push storms *away* from the equator.

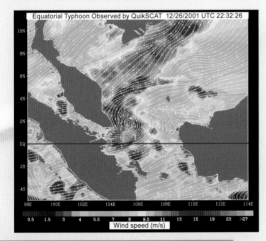

↑ Typhoon Vamei on December 21, 2001. Note that the southern edge of the circulation formed just 85 miles north of the equator. (NASA)

## Tracks and Intensity of All Tropical Storms

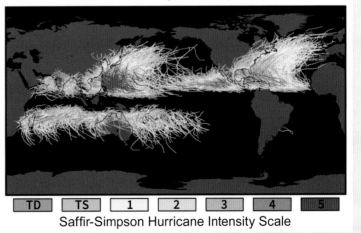

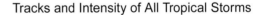

| TD | TS | 1 | 2 | 3 | 4 | 5 |

Saffir-Simpson Hurricane Intensity Scale

↑ A map showing the paths taken by tropical cyclones worldwide. Note that emptiness near the equator. (NASA)

# HOW STORMS INTENSIFY

Once a system achieves tropical storm status, it can work to quickly strengthen—*if* the conditions are right. Storms need two ingredients to strengthen:

→ A satellite map of oceanic heat content in the Atlantic on July 19, 2023. It measures how much energy is stored in warm ocean waters. (NOAA)

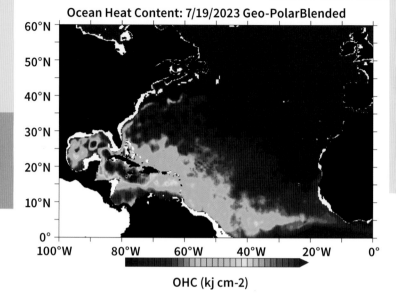

Ocean Heat Content: 7/19/2023 Geo-PolarBlended

OHC (kj cm-2)

## WARM OCEAN WATERS

The hotter the sea surface temperatures, the more **oceanic heat content (OHC)**, or energy, a storm can extract. It's not just how *hot* the water is, though. It's also important how deep that warm water extends. Meteorologists look at the depth of the 26°C (78.8°F) **isotherm**, or water temperature level. During September and October in the Gulf of Mexico, peak hurricane season, that depth might be up to 100 meters (328 feet)—more than a football field—below the surface! Even if a hurricane extracts all the heat energy from surface water, it can upwell, or bring up, warmer waters from below. That influx of warm water sustains it and can even help it to strengthen.

## A LACK OF WIND SHEAR

Wind shear can tear apart a developing storm. Thunderstorms would be pushed and pulled in all directions, preventing them from organizing. That's why hurricanes need weak upper-level winds to form.

When maximum sustained winds near the center of a storm reach 74 mph (119 kph), a storm is declared a hurricane. If winds reach 111 mph (179 kph), it's a major hurricane.

## HOW HURRICANES ARE RATED

In the Atlantic and central and eastern North Pacific, storms are rated on the Saffir-Simpson hurricane wind scale. It originated in 1969, when an engineer named Herbert Saffir was asked by the United Nations to study how to construct inexpensive but resilient homes in hurricane-prone areas. The scale rated hurricanes on a 1 through 5 scale—with 5 being the worst—based on wind speeds.

Saffir gave the scale to the U.S. National Hurricane Center, where the director, Robert Simpson, expanded on it. He added information about the effects of coastal flooding for each category. The scale was debuted to the general public in 1973.

# RAPID INTENSIFICATION

On occasion, a storm strengthens alarmingly quickly. Meteorologists call this **rapid intensification**. It's defined as an increase of 35 mph (56 kph) in a storm's maximum winds in 24 hours or less.

Very rarely, extreme rapid intensification happens at double or even triple that rate. On October 22, 2015, Patricia, a storm in the eastern North Pacific Ocean, intensified faster than any storm ever observed. It exploded from a tropical storm to a Category 5 in a day's time. Maximum sustained winds lurched from 85 mph to 205 mph (137 kph to 330 kph) in 24 hours. Winds later climbed to 215 mph (346 kph)—making it the most powerful storm on record worldwide.

It weakened slightly to Category 4 strength as it moved ashore near Playa Cuixmala, Jalisco, on October 23. Then, its circulation got torn apart by the Sierra Madre Mountains.

Rapid intensification requires the same ingredients as regular strengthening—calm upper-level winds and hot ocean waters are key. But what's *also* useful is a pocket of high pressure in the upper atmosphere *over* a strengthening storm or hurricane.

Aren't highs the opposite of storms? Technically, yes. But high pressure means **divergence**, or the spreading of air. High pressure systems push air away. That can help the **outflow**, or exhaust, exiting a tropical storm or hurricane.

↓ Hurricane Maria at Category 1 strength on September 17, 2017.

↑ Hurricane Maria as a Category 5 just a day later after rapidly intensifying.

The more air fanned away from the *top* of a storm, the more warm, moist air that can rush in from *below* to fuel the storm. Removing air from above a storm also helps reduce how much air is weighing down on the bottom of the storm. That helps the low pressure near the ground intensify, boosting the winds.

Most storms that attain Category 4 or Category 5 status undergo rapid intensification at least once.

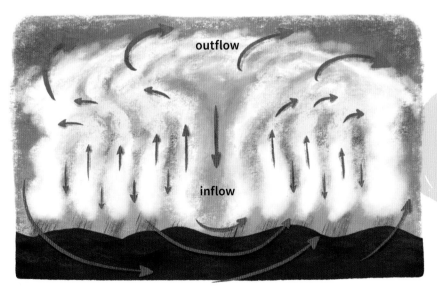

outflow

inflow

The more air evacuated out of the top of a tropical cyclone, the more warm, humid air it can suck in from below.

# THE STORM THAT WASN'T SUPPOSED TO HAPPEN

Tropical cyclones form in most oceans around the world.

One place they don't form is in the South Atlantic Ocean. Winds in the upper atmosphere are too strong. They disrupt a storm before it can organize. And there aren't any disturbances or tropical waves to generate storms to begin with. Besides—water temperatures would be too cool to support the formation of a hurricane anyway.

At least that's what scientists thought—until March of 2004. For days, a non-tropical storm system was lingering off the coast of Brazil. Within this low pressure system, a pocket of thunderstorms formed. Over several days, it acquired tropical characteristics. By March 26, it morphed into a hurricane and even developed an eye—a small circle of calm winds and clear skies in the middle. Hurricane Catarina, the only ever documented South Atlantic hurricane, reached Category 2 strength with 100 mph (161 kph) winds on March 28.

It slammed into the South Region of Brazil at peak strength, damaging 36,000 homes. And it made scientists wonder—could tropical storms or even hurricanes form in the South Atlantic after all?

Researchers later determined that subtropical storms, which have the characteristics of tropical and non-tropical storms, form there an average of once per year. Pure tropical systems remain incredibly rare. Nowadays, the Brazilian Navy Hydrographic Center assigns names to both tropical and subtropical storms.

↑ Hurricane Catarina at peak strength on March 27, 2004. (NASA)

↑ Catarina's path and intensity. (NOAA/Nilfanion/Wikipedia)

# HOW DO STORMS GET NAMES?

Whenever a tropical cyclone develops, it's assigned a name by one of eleven forecast agencies around the world.

In the mid-1800s, tropical systems were only named after hitting. They were usually given nicknames based on the damage they caused.

In 1890, Clement Wragge, an Australian forecaster, became the first person to use a human name to refer to a storm. Before that, he just used Greek letters but then began using women's names. Then, he started picking names of politicians he didn't like.

That practice paused in 1903. Then, in 1944, three U.S. Army Air Force officers in Saipan began naming typhoons after their wives. A year later, the armed services adopted a list of women's names for western Pacific typhoons. In 1947, the practice spread to the Air Force Hurricane Office in Miami, which oversaw storms in the North Atlantic Ocean—but the names weren't used publicly. Storms were only referred to by name within the Air Force.

That changed in 1950, when three hurricanes were present in the Atlantic simultaneously. Tracking them at the same time was a challenge, and the public was confused. Grady Norton, the meteorologist in charge of the U.S. Weather Bureau's Hurricane Warning Center in Miami, decided to use the Air Force's hurricane names in public bulletins. It caught on, and newspapers began picking up the names. In 1978, the World Meteorological Organization asked the Weather Bureau to include both men's and women's names.

Nowadays, the U.S. National Hurricane Center has a rotating list of six sets of names for the Atlantic. They also have one for the Pacific. Each set is organized alphabetically and alternates between male and female names. Every year starts with a new set. Six years later, once all the sets have been burned through, the list starts at the beginning.

If a storm ends up being especially damaging or deadly, however, its name is retired from the list and replaced. That's why there won't ever be another Hurricane Katrina or Hurricane Andrew.

# SUBTROPICAL STORMS

Subtropical storms are a hybrid type of storm that exists on a spectrum in between tropical and non-tropical cyclones. They usually form early or late in hurricane season, when water temperatures are too cool to sustain a fully tropical system. Water temperatures of 75°F (24°C) are usually enough to brew a subtropical storm, whereas fully tropical cyclones thrive on waters above 82°F (28°C).

You can think of a subtropical storm as a tropical storm in the middle of a non-tropical low pressure system. Non-tropical low pressure systems are very large—much bigger than hurricanes. Sometimes, a tiny pocket of thunderstorms can form in the middle of a non-tropical low. If the waters are warm enough, that pocket of thunderstorms can acquire tropical characteristics. Eventually, it might even look like a tropical storm.

In order to be declared subtropical, the central thunderstorm cluster needs to meet the following criteria:

▶ Maximum winds have to be at least 39 mph (63 kph).

▶ The clump of thunderstorms needs to have shedded its fronts—they can't be anchored on any warm or cold fronts.

▶ The storm system has to be "warm core"—deriving most of its energy from warm ocean waters.

▶ Subtropical storms *don't* have a tight doughnut of winds surrounding their centers like tropical cyclones do. With subtropical storms, the winds are more spread out.

▶ If a subtropical storm drifts over warm enough waters, it can become fully tropical. Some can even intensify into hurricanes!

↑ An unnamed subtropical storm in the Atlantic on January 16, 2023. Note the smaller hurricane-like feature at the core of the big swirl of low pressure. (WeatherNerds.org)

## DID YOU KNOW?

Between February 5 and March 14, 2023, Tropical Cyclone Freddy traveled from near Australia to Africa. It hit Madagascar twice! Lasting 37 days, it became the longest-lived named storm in history.

# EXTRATROPICAL TRANSITION

Just like a non-tropical system can *become* a tropical storm or hurricane, the same thing can take place in reverse. That happens when a hurricane or typhoon moves over colder waters. It can also occur when a tropical storm or hurricane begins approaching and feeling the jet stream.

When a hurricane undergoes **extratropical transition**, or gradually becomes non-tropical, a few things happen:

▶ The winds begin to decrease, but they also broaden over a wider area.

▶ The storm starts to extract energy from clashing warm and cold air masses—not warm waters.

▶ Dry air from the mid-latitudes begins to swoosh in behind the system. That causes the storm to take on a comma shape. It loses its classic hurricane symmetry.

▶ Once a hurricane has completed extratropical transition, it is known as **post-tropical**.

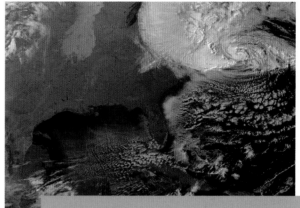

↑ A satellite image of post-tropical Sandy as it hit New Jersey on October 29, 2012. (NOAA)

↑ Damage from Sandy. Notice how much sand has been pushed inland. There is also a home that has been pushed off its foundation. (FEMA)

Post-tropical cyclones don't have winds as strong as tropical systems, but they can be just as dangerous. On October 29, 2012, the extratropical remnants of Hurricane Sandy slammed into New Jersey. Even though it wasn't a hurricane anymore, it packed hurricane-force winds and major coastal flooding. It piled water against the coast at high tide, causing the seas to climb 9 feet (3 m) higher than normal in New York City. A total of 157 people died in the United States. The flooding inundated New York City's subway system and flooded streets and tunnels. The storm knocked out power to 8.2 million households and caused $65 billion in damage.

Part of the reason it was so deadly was because it was so big. Its wind field was 1,000 miles (1,609 km) wide! Moreover, the National Hurricane Center couldn't issue hurricane warnings ahead of its arrival since it wasn't *technically* a hurricane anymore. It was post-tropical.

That made many residents think the storm wasn't serious.

# OTHER HURRICANE-LIKE STORMS

There are other Kona storms worldwide that are *like* hurricanes, but don't quite fit the definition. Here are some examples:

## KONA

Kona storms form in the cool wintertime in the central Pacific Ocean. The term **Kona** means *leeward* in Hawaiian, which describes the direction of the winds during Kona storms. The winds begin out of the southwest and then shift out of the south—trade winds typically come out of the northeast. Kona storms have cold air at their centers, meaning they're not tropical or subtropical. Kona storms frequently bring blizzard conditions to the Hawaiian mountains, mudslides, and severe winds.

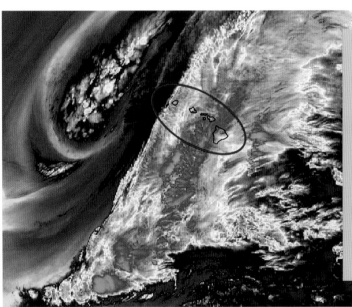

← A Kona low approaches Hawaii on December 6, 2021. Wind gusts of 35 to 50 mph (56 to 80 kph) were common at the lower elevations, and the summit of Mauna Kea, which is 13,801 feet (4,207 m) high, received 6 to 10 inches (15.2 to 25.4 cm) of snow. The storm also dumped 10 to 15 inches (25.4 to 38.1 cm) of rain on the Kana District, located on the south side of the Big Island. Flooding was also reported on several other Hawaiian islands.

# AUSTRALIAN EAST COAST LOWS (ECLS)

Australian East Coast Lows, or ECLs, are storm systems that form offshore of New South Wales and Queensland, Australia, during the late autumn or early winter. They are not tropical, but sometimes show signs of subtropical characteristics. Scientists estimate nearly half of ECLs should be classified as subtropical. ECLs bring heavy rainfall, strong winds, and rough surf.

↑ An Australian east coast low on July 27, 2020, as seen from the Japanese satellite Himawari-8. (Japan Meteorological Agency)

# MEDICANES

Mediterranean hurricanes, or medicanes, aren't exactly hurricanes. The Mediterranean Sea isn't big enough to support the traditional formation of a hurricane. But sometimes, subtropical or even fully tropical low pressure systems can form. Most are weak, with winds between 30 and 50 mph (48 to 80 kph). Some can reach hurricane strength, though. The strongest, which hit in mid-September 2020, produced a wind gust of 120 mph (193 kph) on Cephalonia Island in the Ionian Sea. Named Ianos, it made it as strong as a Category 2 hurricane! Like tropical or subtropical storms, medicanes don't have fronts, and they do sometimes develop eyes. They also form over cooler waters than conventional hurricanes—often between 60 and 75°F (16 and 24°C). Medicanes can be dangerous and bring major coastal flooding, heavy rains, and damaging wind.

↑ A strong medicane, named Ianos, nears Greece at peak intensity on September 17, 2020. It reached Category 2-equivalent strength. (NOAA)

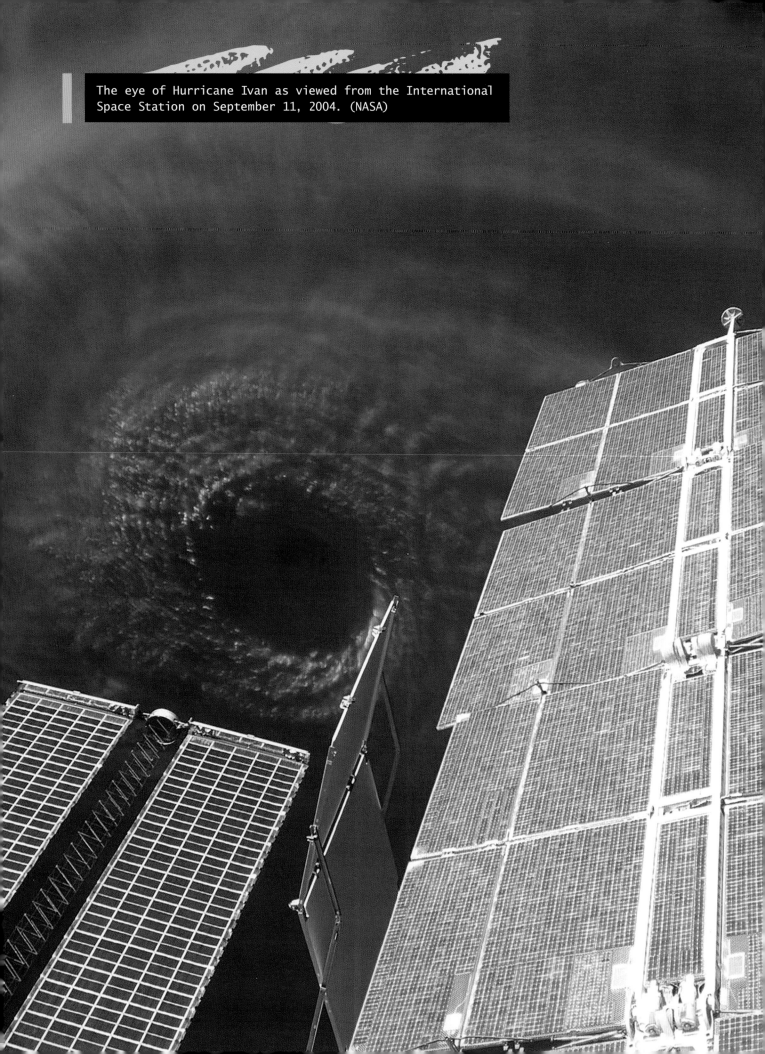

The eye of Hurricane Ivan as viewed from the International Space Station on September 11, 2004. (NASA)

## CHAPTER 6

# INSIDE A HURRICANE

Hurricanes, tropical storms, cyclones, and typhoons occur all around the world. While areas in the tropics are at the greatest risk, tropical systems can impact areas far beyond the tropics too. That's why it's important to be prepared— not scared—and know what to do if a storm is coming.

In the last chapter, we talked about how hurricanes form. In this chapter, we'll venture inside a hurricane. We'll learn about the inner structure of hurricanes, what dangers lurk inside, and how to keep safe.

We'll work together to make a hurricane safety kit. And we'll have a front-row seat looking back at some of my wildest hurricane chases.

Hold onto your hats! It's about to get windy . . .

# WHEN IS HURRICANE SEASON?

Tropical cyclones can form during any season. After all, the atmosphere doesn't own a calendar! As long as the waters are warm enough and upper-level winds are weak, a storm can develop. It's just rarer in the wintertime and early spring.

→ Three hurricanes—Katia, Irma, and Jose—roam the Atlantic simultaneously on September 7, 2017. (NASA)

Each ocean basin has a different storm season. Some are shorter and some are longer. Here's a look at when storms form around the world:

**North Atlantic** hurricane season officially runs from June 1 through November 30. Most storms happen during August, September, and October. On average, September 15 is the peak of hurricane season. In recent years, officials have considered moving the start of Atlantic hurricane season to May 15. That's because warming waters are making preseason storms more common.

**North Pacific** hurricane season has two different start dates. It begins on May 15 in the eastern north Pacific (east of 140 degrees West longitude) and June 1 in the central Pacific (from 140 degrees West to the international date line) and runs through November 30. On average, the eastern Pacific records 15 named storms per season.

**Northwest Pacific** typhoon season stretches from May through October, but realistically storms can—and do—happen any time of year there. An average of 25.9 tropical storms form annually and 16.2 become typhoons. (Typhoons and hurricanes are the same exact thing—they just have different names.)

The **North Indian Ocean** is an unusual place for cyclones. An average of four to six tropical cyclones form there annually. Most of the systems form during April/May or October/November, with a gap during the summertime in between.

**South Pacific** cyclone season runs from November 1 through April 30 (remember that, in the Southern Hemisphere, the seasons are the opposite of the Northern Hemisphere's). An average of seven named storms form, a few of which reach the equivalent of hurricane strength.

In the **Southwest Indian Ocean**, cyclones occur most commonly between November and April. Only December, January, February, and March have recorded **very intense tropical cyclones (VITC)**, which are the highest on the South-West Indian Ocean Tropical Cyclone scale. An average of 9.3 storms form per year in the Southwest Indian Ocean. About half reach hurricane-equivalent strength.

The **South Atlantic Ocean** doesn't have a hurricane season since storms almost never form there. An average of one subtropical cyclone forms there annually.

# ANATOMY OF A HURRICANE

1. Air near the sea surface becomes moist since water is evaporating into it. That warm, humid air outside the hurricane is pulled into the hurricane by its low pressure center.

2. Some of the warm, humid air rises into showers on the edge of the hurricane. We call these showers **spiral rainbands** because they wrap inward toward the storm's center. The rainbands become more intense closer to the middle of the storm.

3. In between spiral rainbands are slots of sinking air. With so much air rising in the hurricane, it has to be sinking somewhere! That subsidence, or sinking motion, leads to calmer conditions in between rainbands.

4. The most intense of the spiral rainbands is the eyewall. In the strongest storms, it forms a perfectly circular ring around the eye. This is where air is rising into the storm the most quickly. The expansion releases heat energy, helping add power to the eyewall. Winds in the eyewall are stronger than anywhere else in the storm.

5. All the warm air that rose in the eyewall reaches the top of the storm. It can't rise through the tropopause, resulting in high pressure. Some of the air fans out sideways. Meteorologists call that **outflow** since it's the exhaust air of the storm. Other pockets of air descend downward in the middle of the storm, eroding the cloud cover. That makes a column of clear, hot, and dry air in the middle of the storm. It's in this area, known as the **eye**, that the winds are calm.

6. The bottom of the eye is where air pressure in the hurricane is the lowest. It's the middle of an atmospheric vacuum. In a strong hurricane, the air in the eye is still. The eyewall, which will bring devastation, surrounds it on all sides.

7. Outflow exiting the hurricane at high altitudes is pushed away from the storm. High in the sky, the air is very cold. That means the clouds are made out of ice crystals.

8. Some of the air sinks back to the surface, where it takes in moisture from the ocean and becomes humid again. It might get sucked back into the storm!

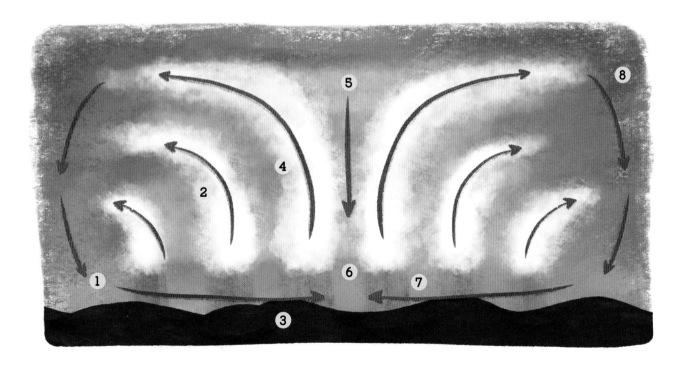

# WHAT IS THE PURPOSE OF HURRICANES?

Every storm and weather system exists to balance heat energy in the atmosphere. Thunderstorms help balance heat vertically by carrying warm air high into the sky and mixing cool air down to the ground. Mid-latitude high pressure and low pressure systems distribute heat horizontally. Hurricanes and tropical cyclones transport heat from the tropics to the polar regions.

Even long after a hurricane has dissipated, it leaves behind a blob of warm air. Most of this leftover warm air gets swept up by the jet stream. That causes warming.

↑ Super Typhoon Haiyan on November 7, 2013, nearing the Philippines. (NOAA/CIRA)

## BIGGEST, STRONGEST, AND FASTEST

**Biggest:** Typhoon Tip in the Pacific in October, 1979. 1,380 miles (2,221 km) wide. Tip was a Category 5–equivalent violent typhoon. Hurricane-force winds spread out 250 miles (402 km) from the center!

**Smallest:** Tropical Storm Marco in the Bay of Campeche on October 7, 2008. Maximum winds reached 65 mph (105 kph), but tropical storm–force winds only reached 11.5 miles (18.5 km) outward from the center.

**Lowest air pressure:** Typhoon Tip on October 12, 1979. Air pressure of 870 millibars (normal air pressure is 1015 millibars). That meant 13 percent of the atmosphere was "missing" from the storm's center, driving its strong winds.

**Strongest winds:** Hurricane Patricia, offshore of Mexico in the Pacific, on October 23, 2015. Winds estimated at 215 mph (346 kph).

A comparison of the sizes of Typhoon Tip and Tropical Storm Marco. (NOAA)

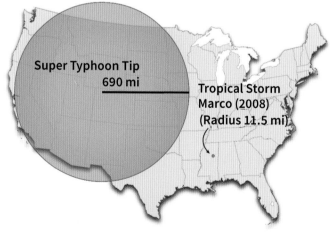

Super Typhoon Tip
690 mi

Tropical Storm Marco (2008) (Radius 11.5 mi)

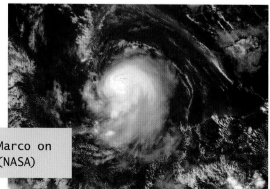

→ Tropical Storm Marco on October 6, 2008. (NASA)

# MOTHER NATURE'S HEAT ENGINES

Hurricanes and tropical cyclones are heat machines. In fact, they're a lot like engines. The way they work is similar!

Air from outside the storm is warmed by toasty ocean waters below. That air is drawn toward the center of the storm.

As the air pressure drops inside the storm, however, air pockets expand. That means they grow in *volume*. That expansion releases heat energy, which powers the storm. It also causes the air pocket to cool down. The moisture in the air pocket condenses into raindrops, which then fall out of the clouds.

But here's what makes hurricanes so fierce. Ordinarily, this process would harvest *all* the heat energy out of the air pocket. By the time it got to the middle of the storm, it wouldn't have any energy left, and the storm would fall apart.

But with a hurricane, the air pocket is *constantly* being reheated and ingesting more moisture from the hot ocean waters below. It's warmed at the exact rate it would otherwise cool from expanding. And it's energized at the same rate it's giving energy to the storm. As long as the storm is over warm water, it can rage on. (That's also why hurricanes usually fall apart after they move over land).

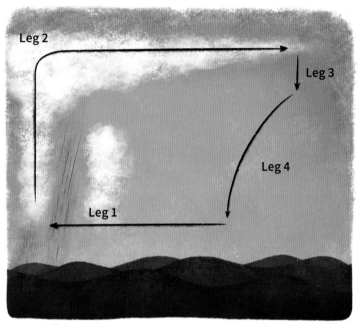

Leg 1: Air is warmed by hot ocean.
Leg 2: Air is cooled by expansion.
Leg 3: Air dries, releasing heat to environment.
Leg 4: Air sinks and warms.

## DID YOU KNOW?

It's estimated that one-fifteenth, or between 6 and 7 percent, of all the heat energy carried to the poles is done by hurricanes.

# OTHER HURRICANE HAZARDS

Hurricanes aren't *just* big buzzsaws of wind. They have lots of other dangers too—even far from the center of the storm. Let's break down some of the common threats.

## STORM SURGE

When a hurricane approaches land, onshore winds push water toward the coast. This forces the ocean to spill onto land and can cause devastating flooding.

How bad a storm's surge is depends on two factors: the storm's *strength* and *size*. If a storm has stronger winds, it will shove more water onto land. And bigger storms mean a bigger surge. The shape of the ocean floor can also affect storm surge. A flatter, shallower ocean bottom makes it easier for a storm to generate a huge surge.

Storm surge can sometimes mean water rising 20 feet (6 m) or more above ordinarily dry ground. That's why officials urge coastal residents to evacuate and move inland.

Storms can also suck water *away* from the coast. This occurs on the side of the storm with offshore winds. Tampa Bay was partially emptied ahead of Hurricane Irma in September 2017. The ocean floor was exposed!

wind

storm surge

## DID YOU KNOW?

In the Northern Hemisphere, hurricanes spin counterclockwise. That means the worst flooding will be to the *right* of the storm's center. In the Southern Hemisphere, the worst flooding will be to the *left* of the center.

↑ Storm surge damage in Gilchrist, Texas, left by Hurricane Ike in 2008. (Jocelyn Augusitno/FEMA)

# HEAVY RAINFALL

Hurricanes are extremely wet storms. The entire air mass within a hurricane is saturated—that means it can't hold any more water. The extra water falls out of the air as rain, and there's *a lot* of it. Rainfall rates can easily exceed 4 inches (10 cm) per hour in hurricanes.

It's common for hurricanes to dump 10, 20, or even 30 inches (25, 51, or 76 cm) of rain wherever they hit. The heavy totals can reach far from the core of the hurricane. In fact, some regions that never even *see* the hurricane can tap into its moisture.

That's what happens during PREs, or **predecessor rain events**. Moisture streaming away from the equator and *ahead* of a storm can trigger flash flooding. PREs happen when that moisture pools along a cold front. The cold front creates downpours and thunderstorms, which convert the moist air into extreme rainfall.

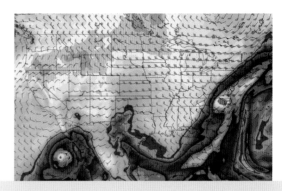

↑ Weather models simulate moisture wafting north ahead of Hurricane Michael in mid-October 2018. (College of DuPage NEXLAB)

→ Flooding in Port Arthur, Texas, on August 31, 2017, produced by Hurricane Harvey's remnants. (South Carolina National Guard)

# TORNADOES

Hurricanes and tropical storms routinely produce tornadoes. Most form on the outer edges of the storm in the spiral rainbands.

Wind near the ground slows down, but winds aloft keep blowing strong. That wind shear helps columns of circulation to form rain showers within the spiral rainbands that can rotate. Any of them can produce tornadoes.

Some tropical cyclones produce no tornadoes, while others spawn dozens. Hurricane Ivan in 2004 generated 120 tornadoes! Buelah in 1967 dropped 117 twisters.

↑ Damage from an F1 tornado in Stewartsville, Virginia. The tornado happened as the remnants of Hurricane Ivan passed through the eastern United States on September 17, 2004. (NWS Blacksburg, VA)

# INSIDE THE EYEWALL

The eyewall is the most intense part of a hurricane. Wind speeds can exceed 160 mph (258 kph) in the strongest eyewalls. Some hurricane eyewalls are up to 9.5 miles (15 km) tall.

A hurricane's eyewall surrounds its eye. In the eyewall, air is moving quickly upward. It's also spinning rapidly around the eye. That air doesn't *enter* the eye, however, which is the secret to why the winds are so strong. That's because the eyewall is in **cyclostrophic balance**.

What does *that* mean!? Well, we know air is being vacuumed toward the eye of the hurricane. That's because of the low pressure's powerful suction. But, as it swirls around and around the eye, it's also being pushed *outward* by centrifugal force. (That's the same force that flings you outward when you take a sharp turn in the car.) Those two forces are in perfect balance.

The quicker the pressure drops close to the storm's center, the faster the winds. It's like skiing. The steeper the slope, or drop-off, of the hill, the faster you'll go.

If air could enter the eye and "fill in" the zone of low pressure, the storm would dissipate. That's why, in order to survive, the hurricane has to spin fast enough to maintain the outward push of the centrifugal force. It's just like stirring a cup of coffee—if you want the coffee to dip in the middle (that dip represents low pressure), you have to be stirring quickly!

Outside the eyewall, there's usually a relative lull in the wind. But when it hits, winds spike abruptly. The wind speeds are often as strong as a tornado. Rain falls so heavily that it becomes impossible to see. Pinpoint lightning strikes accompany the strongest eyewalls.

Every couple of days (sometimes more), a hurricane undergoes an **eyewall replacement cycle**. The eyewall becomes oblong in shape, shrivels up, and disintegrates as it falls into the eye. A new eyewall forms around it and contracts toward the middle, taking the old one's place.

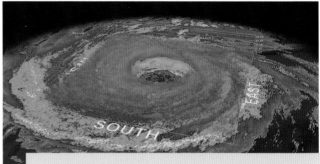

↑ A three-dimensional radar view of the eye of Hurricane Harvey approaching Rockport, Texas, on August 26, 2017.

↑ A radar view of Hurricane Andrew's eyewall on August 24, 1992, in South Florida.

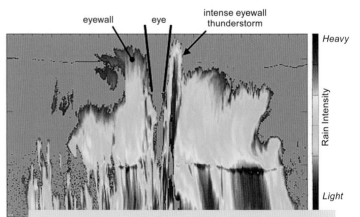

↑ A slice through Hurricane Emily in 2005. The eyewall was nearly 60,000 feet (18,288 m) tall. (NASA)

# MESOVORTICES

**Mesovortices** are broad swirls a few miles (kilometers) across that form within the eyewall. Usually, only four or five can fit within the eye. They form because of the extreme gradient, or change with distance, of winds on the inside of the eyewall. It's difficult for the atmosphere to transition from extreme wind to calm so quickly! That's why smaller eddies develop where the inner edge of the eyewall meets the eye.

Mesovortices themselves aren't violent types of wind. They're weak circulations. But they bend and contort the eyewall and make its inner edge wavy. That makes for wild fluctuations of air pressure and wind as the eye arrives. Winds may go calm and you might *think* you're safely in the eye. Then, *BAM!* A piece of the eyewall rotates through and hits you with a 100 mph (161 kph) wind gust.

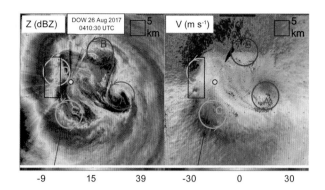

↑ Mesovortices in the eye of Hurricane Harvey on the night of August 25–26, 2017, in South Texas. The image came from a highly sensitive mobile Doppler radar, which was mounted on a truck. (Kosiba, K. & Wurman, J. [2018]. The Role of Small-Scale Vortices in Enhancing Surface Winds and Damage in Hurricane Harvey. *Monthly Weather Review*, *146*[3]. https://doi.org/10.1175/MWR-D-17-0327.1)

# ROLL VORTICES

The presence of very fast wind blowing over slightly slower wind causes air pockets to tumble over each other. That makes **roll vortices**, or elongated tubes of overturning air. On the downward side of a roll vortex, winds in the storm are enhanced. That can cause more damage.

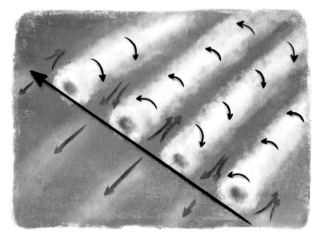

**Downward-moving air pulls down stronger winds**　　**Upward-moving air, slightly lesser winds**

# TORNADOES AND MINI-SWIRLS

Tornadoes occasionally form in the eyewall of hurricanes. **Mini-swirls**, however, are more common.

Mini-swirls are different from tornadoes. Tornadoes begin in a cloud and spin down to the ground. Mini-swirls are a different type of vortex, similar in size to a small tornado, that begin near the ground and spin upward.

They're started by small eddies or whirls that develop as air blows around an object. Strong winds just above the ground stretch that pocket of spin vertically. That makes a vertical vortex.

Mini-swirls might be a few tens of feet (meters) wide and several hundred feet (kilometers) tall— *much* smaller than a typical tornado. Their wind speeds are lower too, and they don't last very long—probably only a few seconds to around a minute. But their winds can combine with the background winds in the hurricane itself to cause narrow strips of extra-intense damage.

# THE EYE

The eye is an oasis of calm in the middle of a hurricane. The winds weaken, and the air is usually wam and dry. Sometimes, dry sinking air punches all the way to the ground, preventing cloud cover. The eyes in even the most monstrous hurricanes can be clear. It's like being in the center of an atmospheric whirlpool.

If you're standing in the eye, you may be able to spot the **stadium effect**—towering clouds from the eyewall surrounding you in all directions. The front half of the storm has already passed, leaving a mess of damage all around. The back of the storm—beginning with the eyewall—is still coming.

Before people understood how hurricanes worked, many would venture out into the eye, assuming the storm was over. They didn't realize they were only halfway done.

Most eyes are 20 to 40 miles (32 to 64 km) wide. Some are only a mile or two (1.6 to 3.2 km) wide.

↑ The Air Force Reserve Hurricane Hunters fly through the eye of Hurricane Dorian in September of 2019. (U.S. Air Force)

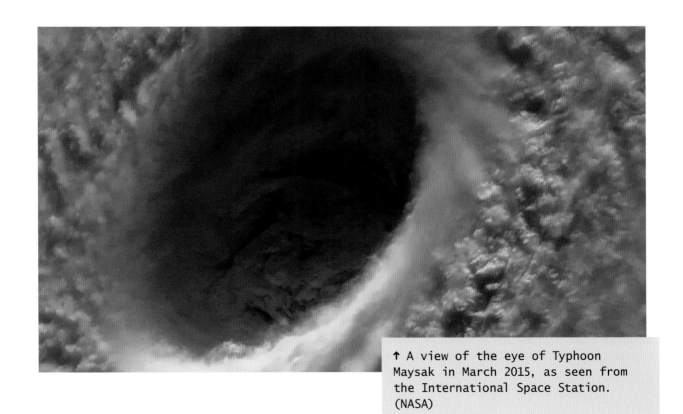

↑ A view of the eye of Typhoon Maysak in March 2015, as seen from the International Space Station. (NASA)

# BROWN OCEAN EFFECT

Hurricane Andrew was a small yet potent Category 5 hurricane that hit South Florida on August 24, 1992. It began as a tropical depression over the eastern Atlantic on August 16. It remained a weak storm until August 23, when it rapidly intensified into a Category 5 as it neared the Bahamas.

The storm carved through Miami-Dade County, damaging more than 124,000 homes and destroying 63,000 others. In Biscayne Bay, strong winds pushed water toward the coast. Water levels reached 6 feet (2 m) above normal. A house in Perrine County, Florida had an anemometer that measured a wind gust to 177 mph (285 kph). The National Hurricane Center's office in Coral Gables—where forecasts and warnings originate—recorded a gust of 164 mph (264 kph). Then, the anemometer broke. Key Largo, Florida, experienced 13 minutes of winds sustained at 114 mph (183 kph).

Andrew's size and swift movement limited how much rainfall occurred. But, in addition to the scores of mini-swirls and tornadoes that accompanied Andrew's passage, something else strange happened—Andrew didn't *weaken* after hitting land. In fact, it maintained strength and even intensified.

Why didn't Andrew diminish? It's because of something called the **brown ocean effect**. Basically, if a hurricane passes over warm, wet soils or swampland, it thinks it's still over the ocean. The storm extracts heat energy from evaporating moisture, allowing it to continue. That's how Hurricane Andrew remained a Category 5 as it swirled over the entire South Florida peninsula—it was passing over the Everglades.

↓ A nursing home damaged by Erin's high winds in Caddo County, Oklahoma, on August 20, 2005. (FEMA)

↑ Tropical Storm Erin intensifies over Oklahoma on August 19, 2007. (NOAA/NWS)

Tropical Storm Erin exhibited a similar surprise intensification in 2007. It made landfall in Texas as a weak storm with 40 mph (64 kph) on August 16. Its remnants swirled inland, gradually weakening. But then something unexpected happened. It quickly strengthened over Oklahoma. Sustained winds reached 60 mph (97 kph). A wind gust of 82 mph (132 kph) was recorded in the town of Watonga.

"An extraordinary weather event continues to unfold over central Oklahoma early this morning as the remnants of Tropical Storm Erin have intensified . . . resulting in what amounts to an inland tropical storm," wrote the National Weather Service in Norman, Oklahoma, on August 19. The town of Eakly recorded 12.81 inches (152.40 cm) of rain.

Scientists found a few key ingredients that makes the brown ocean effect possible. First, the lower atmosphere has to be uniform in temperature. Second, soils have to be saturated—or filled—with warm water. And third, that soil has to contain at least one-third as much available latent heat as warm ocean waters.

Therefore, hurricanes don't *always* weaken when they move ashore!

# MAKE A HURRICANE KIT

Hurricanes can strengthen quickly, and forecasters sometimes struggle to predict where they'll hit. Authorities may choose to order evacuations, encouraging residents to temporarily move away from the coastline. That's when a collection of ready supplies, a **hurricane kit,** comes in handy.

## HERE ARE SOME SUGGESTED NECESSITIES:

+ Water (one gallon [4 L] per person per day for at least 3 days)
+ Food (canned and nonperishable)
+ Batteries
+ Flashlight
+ First aid kit
+ Medications
+ Toiletries (toothbrush, toothpaste, and soap)
+ Whistle (to signal for help)
+ Dust masks (in case air becomes polluted)
+ Garbage bags and plastic ties
+ Wrench or pliers (to turn off leaking pipes)
+ Maps
+ Cell phone chargers and extra batteries
+ Infant food/diapers
+ Pet food and supplies
+ Cash
+ Sleeping bag
+ Changes of clothes
+ Matches in a waterproof container
+ Paper/pencil
+ Toilet paper and paper towels

Gather all your provisions and store your hurricane kit in an out-of-the-way but accessible place so it will be ready if you ever need it.

⚠ Make sure to let the rest of your family know its whereabouts.

A winter storm dumps heavy snow in Massachusetts.

## CHAPTER 7

# WINTER STORMS AND BLIZZARDS

Snowstorms and blizzards are some of the wildest weather events on the planet. Snow can pile several feet (meters) high, winds can rage like in a hurricane, and it can be impossible to see anything outside.

Winter is a season experienced near the poles and at the mid-latitudes. In the tropics, where it's warm year-round, winter isn't very noticeable. The weather changes slightly, but it doesn't get very cold. Snow also doesn't happen, except in the mountains.

At the mid-latitudes, however, winter can be harsh. Temperatures plummet, a cold wind blows, and most of the leaves fall off the trees and die. The days become shorter and the nights darker.

In this chapter, we'll learn why winter happens. We'll discuss what changes take place in the atmosphere, why winter storms happen, and what makes them so powerful.

# WHAT IS WINTER?

**W**inter is defined differently depending on who you ask.

Astronomical winter has to do with the position of the planets. It begins on the *winter solstice*, or the shortest day of the year. That's when the sun's most direct rays are farthest away. That means long nights and lots of darkness. It's why temperatures get cooler. Astronomical winter lasts until the *vernal equinox*—the first day of spring.

Meteorological winter is a more basic term that meteorologists use. It's just the coldest three calendar months of the year. In the Northern Hemisphere, that's December, January, and February. In the Southern Hemisphere, it's June, July, and August.

↑ My younger sister, Emily, during a snowstorm in 2009. The snow was taller than she was! (She is still short.)

## WHAT HAPPENS IN THE WINTERTIME?

Not only do the days get shorter in the wintertime, but the *intensity* of the sunlight decreases. That's because the sun is shining from a lower point in the sky. It's forced to spread its warming rays over a broader area. That means any given location experiences less heating.

Because of this, the blob of frigid air over the Arctic (or Antarctic) begins to grow. Polar night sets in. That's the name given to the months of darkness that affect regions around the North Pole or South Pole. At either pole, there are 179 days a year when the sun never shines! That leads to *bitterly* cold temperatures.

This cold air expands toward the equator. In the Northern Hemisphere, cold air descends over North America, Europe, northern Africa, and most of Asia. When the Southern Hemisphere faces its version of winter, temperatures drop in South America and Australia, as well as southern Africa.

The influx, or arrival, of cold air shoves warmer air closer to the equator. That causes a bunched-up zone of clashing temperature—where cold and warm air meet. That happens between the tropics and the poles, in the mid-latitudes.

The jet stream moves closer to the equator. It tries to follow the region of opposing temperatures. Meteorologist call this a baroclinic zone. It's a chaotic temperature battleground known for brewing powerful storms.

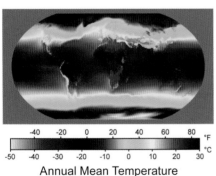

Annual Mean Temperature

↑ A map of average annual temperature. Storm systems form in the baroclinic zones, or the zones where temperature changes quickly with distance. (Robert A. Rohde, edited)

# WHAT'S A POLAR VORTEX?

A **polar vortex** is a whirlpool of extremely cold air. It's anchored over the North Pole or South Pole. The frigid air is dense, so it sinks closer to the ground. That creates a vacuum in the upper atmosphere that pulls in more air. That air cools down and continues the process. As air spirals into the vortex, it curves east due to the Coriolis force.

There are actually *two* polar vortexes (vortices) in the Northern Hemisphere and two in the Southern Hemisphere. They're stacked on top of each other.

The **tropospheric polar vortex** is closest to the ground. It's present year-round. Temperatures aren't as cold, and the vortex isn't strong. The edge of the tropospheric polar vortex is wonky and wavy. The jet stream weaves around the edge of the tropospheric polar vortex.

The **stratospheric polar vortex** is stronger. It's located high above the ground in the **stratosphere**, or the second layer of the atmosphere. The stratospheric polar vortex forms each autumn, strengthening during the coldest, darkest days of winter. Then, it dissipates every spring.

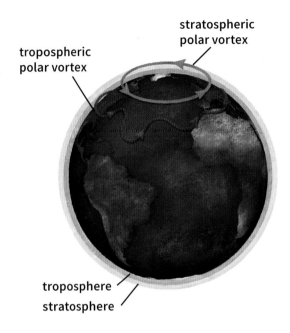

The stratospheric polar vortex is like a buzzsaw of cold. It's circular and has a smooth edge. When it's strong, it spins *fast*. That bottles up all the cold air over the Arctic (or Antarctic). But if it weakens or is knocked out of balance, it unleashes its frigid air. That can bring winter weather outbreaks to the mid-latitudes.

Imagine you're stirring a glass of chocolate milk. If you spin more vigorously, the milk swirls faster, and the fluid in the middle dips. That simulates a *strong vortex*. But if you spin slower or jostle the glass, the dip in the middle fills in—and milk sloshes to the edge. That's how the *weak* stratospheric polar vortex works.

Sometimes, a **sudden stratospheric warming (SSW)** occurs. That's when something happens to disrupt the stratospheric polar vortex. The vortex abruptly warms up. That displaces the cold air away from the pole, pushing cold pockets toward the equator and bringing wild winter weather with it.

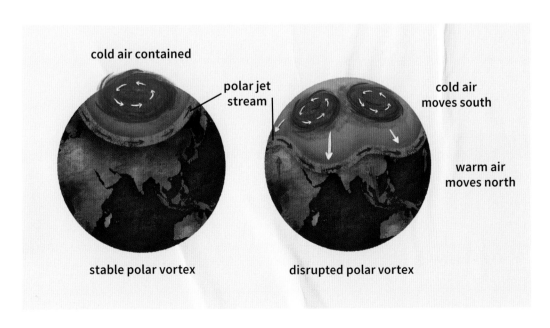

# WINTER STORMS

The most powerful winter storms come from low pressure systems that form when warm and cold air meet. They feed off energy from the jet stream. The warm air brings moisture, and the cold air makes it fall as snow.

For a storm to deliver wintry precipitation, temperatures must be near or below freezing. If the air is too warm, only rain will fall.

Stronger low pressure systems also bring stronger winds. That means that heavy snow can combine with icy gusts. That can kick up snow and reduce **visibility**, or how far you can see. A **whiteout** happens when you can't see anything—just blowing snow!

When that happens, the storm may become a **blizzard**. That's defined as three hours of blowing or falling snow, 35 mph (56 kph) winds, *and* visibilities below a quarter mile (402 m). If you go outside during a blizzard, you might become lost or disoriented. You should never drive or venture outdoors in blizzard conditions.

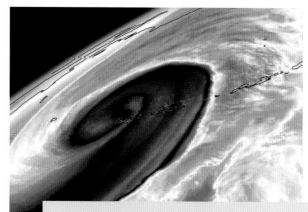

↑ A winter storm over the Alaskan Aleutian Islands on December 12, 2015. (CIMSS)

## CAN IT SNOW ABOVE FREEZING?

Yes! If the air is dry. That's because of something called **evaporative cooling**.

When a snowflake melts, its edges turn to water. When the air is dry, that water evaporates. But, as it evaporates, it sucks heat from the remainder of the snowflake. That can help chill what's left of the flake and keep it below freezing.

## DID YOU KNOW?

Technically, snow could still reach the surface even if air temperatures were in the 50s. On April 28, 1988, Washington, D.C., recorded snow at 48°F (9°C)!

# BOMB CYCLONES

A **bomb cyclone** is an especially mighty winter storm. Bomb cyclones start like ordinary low pressure systems, but then explosively intensify. That can happen because of the arrival of jet stream energy, or a potent high-altitude weather system can strengthen it. Whatever the case, the intensification is *quick*.

Most bomb cyclones have hurricane-force winds. Some even whip up gusts of 100 mph (161 kph). On rare occasions, the storms even develop an eye.

Storms usually become bomb cyclones over the open ocean. On average, the Northern Hemisphere records 45 bomb cyclones per year. The Southern Hemisphere gets about 26.

In addition to heavy precipitation and strong winds, bomb cyclones can cause a coastal storm surge. That means they push water against the shoreline, causing flooding. Sometimes, the surge can be as much as 6 to 9 feet (2 to 3 m).

↑ A bomb cyclone on January 4, 2018. (NOAA)

Temperatures also crash behind a bomb cyclone. That's because the storm swirls cold air toward the equator in its wake. No wonder they can lead to epic snow totals! It can also push a cold front, or band of cold air, all the way into the tropics, resulting in severe thunderstorms and tornadoes.

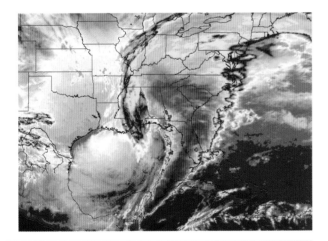

↑ A satellite image of the Storm of the Century on March 13, 1993.

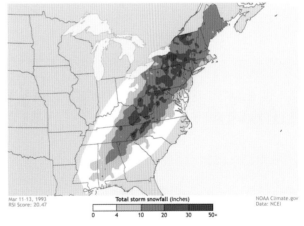

↑ A map of snowfall produced by the Storm of the Century. (NOAA/NCEI)

# SNOW SQUALLS

↑ A snow squall in early 2014. (Matthew Cappucci)

Snow squalls form along cold fronts. Moisture ahead of the front is kicked upward by dry, frigid air, creating a band of snow showers.

The setup is the same recipe that makes downpours and thunderstorms in the summertime. But since it's so cold, the precipitation falls as *heavy* snow.

The arrival of a snow squall is quick. The weather goes from pleasant to whiteout conditions in seconds. Visibility drops to a few hundred feet (meters). Winds gust over 35 mph (56 kph).

Snow squalls aren't usually dangerous unless you're driving. Then, the abrupt drop in visibility can prove fatal. On March 28, 2022, a snow squall in Pennsylvania triggered a deadly 80-car pileup. Six people died and 24 people were injured. Another horrible wreck caused by a snow squall happened on January 9, 2015, in Climax, Michigan. There were 193 vehicles involved. One person was killed. A semi-truck leaked fuel, causing a fire that ignited a truck filled with 40,000 pounds (18,144 kg) of fireworks. The stranded accident victims had to dive for cover.

↑ A weather-related crash on Oregon Highway 22 in the Cascades Mountains on February 24, 2009. (Oregon Department of Transportation)

⚠ Nowadays, in the United States, the National Weather Service issues warnings ahead of snow squalls. It's a way to convince drivers to pull to the side of the road—and stay alive.

# LAKE-EFFECT SNOW

Lake-effect snow is extremely localized, but intense. It happens when cold air blows over warmer waters. Moisture from the lake evaporates and then forms a band of snow clouds. Once those clouds move inland, they dump piles of snow.

Lake-effect snowstorms are common during the late autumn and winter before the lake waters have cooled down. The bigger the difference in temperature between a body of water and the air above, the more water evaporates into the air—and the more snow that's created!

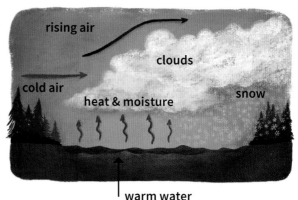

rising air

clouds

cold air

heat & moisture

snow

warm water

# SNOW MADNESS IN BUFFALO

↑ Aftermath of up to 5 feet (2 m) of snow in south Buffalo, New York, on November 17, 2014. (Anthony Quintano)

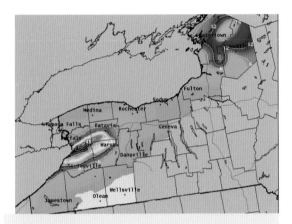

↑ Snowfall during the first half of the storm. Notice how dramatic the change in snowfall over a short distance is. (NWS Buffalo)

Between November 13 and 26, 2014, back-to-back lake-effect snow bands pummeled parts of western New York. Cold air, with temperatures of 20 to 30°F (-7 to -1°C) degrees, was blowing over Lake Erie. The lake's water temperature was 48.7°F (9.3°C) degrees.

The snow fell at a rate of up to 9 inches (23 cm) per hour. Thunder and lightning happened at the same time as the snow. A total of 88 inches (224 cm)—more than 7 feet (2 m)— was reported in East Aurora, New York. Hamburg got 79.5 inches (201.9 cm), and West Seneca had 78 inches (198 cm). At least 24 people died, mostly from heart attacks while shoveling. Thousands of drivers became stranded in the snow.

Lake-effect snows are common in the United States and Canada around the Great Lakes. A similar process called **ocean-effect snow** also happens around the world.

Georgia, Romania, Bulgaria, and northern Turkey sometimes see snow from cold air blowing over the Black Sea. Iran gets it from the Caspian Sea, and even the Adriatic Sea produces occasional snow bands in Italy!

The Japanese Alps get incredible amounts of ocean-effect snow each year. That's because cold Siberian air blows over the warmer Sea of Japan. Some places get 120 feet (37 m) or more per year!

# THE STRANGEST THINGS TO PRODUCE SNOW

Mother Nature's normal methods aren't the only ways to make snowfall. Sometimes, snow pops up in strange ways. Here's a list of weird things that have made snow:

**Airplanes:** On November 27, 2018, airplanes landing at Chicago's O'Hare International Airport produced light snow. The airplanes were flying through clouds at the time. The dirty exhaust from the airplane engines acted as little seeds that ice crystals formed on. It happened again in Dallas, Texas, on February 12, 2021.

**Power plants:** If the air is cold enough, steam from power plants can turn into snow. On January 23, 2013, steam from the Beaver Valley Nuclear Power Station near Shippingport, Pennsylvania, produced 1 inch (2.5 cm) of snow. It happened in Ohio and Wisconsin as well in 2018.

**Rivers:** On the morning of November 12, 2019, flurries fell in Memphis, Tennessee. Why? Cold air was blowing down the Mississippi River. Just like lake-effect snow, that created a tiny band of light snow.

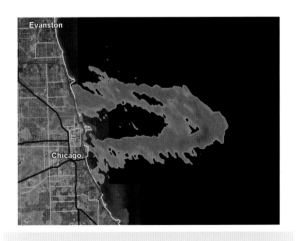

↑ Airplane-effect snow over Chicago in 2018.

# THUNDERSNOW

**Y**es, thundersnow is real. It's exactly what it sounds like—thunder and lightning during a snowstorm.

Thunder and lightning form when warm air rises and makes thunderclouds. But, if it's cold enough to snow, there isn't much warm air rising! That's why thundersnow is so rare. To get thundersnow, air near the ground needs to be warm enough to rise, but cold enough for snow.

Hearing thundersnow is special. That's because snow muffles the sound of the thunder. So even if there *is* lightning and thunder, you only hear it if it's *very* close by.

Just like in summer thunderstorms, the lightning is still dangerous. People have been injured or even killed by thundersnow. On February 23, 2002, lightning struck a hill in Caribou, Maine, where four boys were sledding. One was critically injured and hospitalized.

There's one *other* way thundersnow forms—but it's rarer. Tubes of cool air can climb *diagonally* in a large-scale storm system and produce thunder and lightning. Meteorologists call that **slantwise convection**. It requires a very complex and unusual set of conditions to develop.

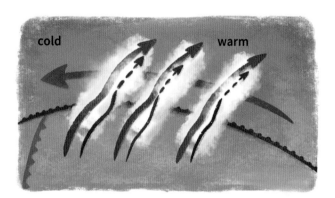

## DID YOU KNOW?

Lots of thundersnow is actually manmade. Tall towers and skyscrapers can help focus charge, or electrical energy, in clouds that sparks a lightning bolt! Sometimes, the cloud's electricity is too weak to make a lightning bolt on its own, but it gets bolstered by human-made structures.

## OTHER TYPES OF WINTRY PRECIPITATION

There are other types of precipitation that form in the wintertime too.

**Sleet** is made up of small ice pellets. It happens when snowflakes fall through a shallow layer of warm air and melt. But then they refreeze into little bits of ice before reaching the surface. Sleet pellets bounce when they hit the ground. If you walk on them, you might hear a *crunch*!

**Freezing rain** is the most dangerous form of precipitation. Raindrops fall as liquid, but freeze when they hit a cold layer on the ground. That transforms the surface into a sheet of ice.

Freezing rain commonly is often the result of **overrunning**. That means warm, moist air "runs over" a layer of cold air closer to the ground. On exceptional occasions, the freezing rain can last for days. That can leave a coating of ice 2 inches (5 cm) thick! Meteorologists call this an **ice storm**. Power lines fall under the weight of the ice, driving becomes impossible, and tree branches collapse, ruining forests.

**Freezing fog** is sneaky and dangerous. It *looks* like regular fog and forms the same way, but at temperatures below freezing. It requires supercooled water droplets—tiny drops of water that rain as liquid even at air temperatures below freezing. If the air is clean, the droplets have nothing to freeze onto. But if a droplet touches anything on the ground, it freezes instantly. That can cause ice and dangerous driving, even if no actual precipitation is falling.

**A diagram outlining how different temperature profiles (layers) can cause different types of wintry precipitation.**

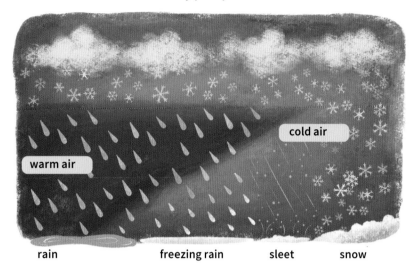

rain · · · · · · · · · · · freezing rain · · · · · sleet · · · · · snow

# STING JETS

Mid-latitude low pressure systems, or cyclones, are known for producing strong winds. But sometimes a "stinger" of extreme winds can appear on their back sides.

Meteorologists only learned about **sting jets** during the Great Storm of 1987, which struck Europe. On the night of October 15–16, hurricane-force winds slammed France and the United Kingdom. Twenty-two people died. Winds gusted to 135 mph (217 kph) in Pointe Du Roc, Granville, France, and 120 mph (193 kph) in Shoreham-by-Sea, West Sussex, in the United Kingdom.

What was the problem? Nobody predicted it. On the evening of October 15, most TV and radio weather forecasts called for heavy rain. They mentioned breezy winds. But they never expected damaging or destructive gusts.

So what happened? Strong winds from the upper atmosphere wrapped around the storm's center. They dragged moist air into a region of dry air. That caused the moisture to evaporate, which dried out the air. Since dry air is denser, or heavier, than moist air, the air sank. And that pulled extreme winds over 100 mph (161 kph) to the surface.

Nowadays, meteorologists know how to look for sting jets. They can sometimes predict them in advance. If not, they can spot them using satellite pictures.

Most of the time, sting jets happen over the ocean. But when they impact land, the results are bad.

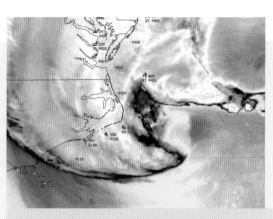

↑ The GOES East weather satellite captures a sting jet in a storm off the U.S. East Coast on January 4, 2018. (CIMSS)

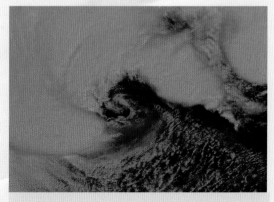

↑ Another view of the same sting jet as seen from the Suomi National Polar-Orbiting Partnership (NPP) satellite. (CIMSS)

# SNOW CRYSTAL STRUCTURES

Some snow is wet and heavy. Other snow is light and fluffy. Why? Different temperatures make different **crystal structures** of snowflakes.

Meteorologists talk about the **snow-to-liquid ratio** of snow a lot. That's a fancy way of saying, "How much water does it take to make this snow?"

With temperatures near freezing, 1 inch (2.5 cm) of water would make 10 inches (25 cm) of snow. But as temperatures get colder, the **fluff factor** goes up. At temperatures around 15°F (-9°C) , 1 inch (2.5 cm) of water could make 30 inches (76 cm) of snow!

Here's how *you* can calculate the snow-to-liquid ratio.

## THE SCIENCE BEHIND THE FUN:

When temperatures are near freezing, snowflakes tend to clump together. They can be a bit wetter. That clumping makes the snowpack denser and thicker. When the air is cold, though, individual ice crystals stack atop each other. This causes them to fluff up more. Different types of ice crystals also form at different temperatures.

1. Once the ground is covered in snow, scoop some snow into the cup. *Don't push it down or crush it.* We want to preserve its natural fluffiness.

2. Measure the height of the cup. Record this number.

3. Go inside and let the snow melt.

4. Measure how high the watermark is inside the cup.

Perhaps you *started* with 6 inches (15 cm) of snow, but now you only have half an inch (13 mm) of water. That means you have a 12:1 snow-to-liquid ratio—1 inch (2.5 cm) of water would give you 12 inches (30 cm) of snow. Using the data you collected, try calculating your own snow-to-liquid ratio!

## HERE'S WHAT YOU'LL NEED:

+ Freshly fallen snow
+ Ruler
+ Cup

↓ A diagram showing which types of crystals tend to form at different combinations of temperature and humidity.

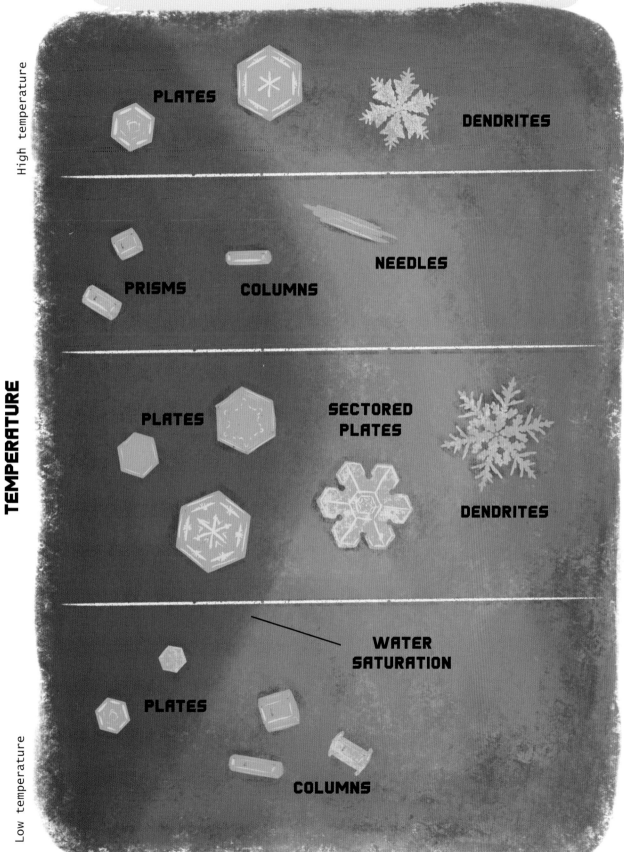

**TEMPERATURE**

High temperature

Low temperature

PLATES

DENDRITES

PRISMS    COLUMNS

NEEDLES

PLATES    SECTORED PLATES

DENDRITES

WATER SATURATION

PLATES

COLUMNS

Low humidity    **HUMIDITY**    High humidity

A delicate purple sunset near Cole, Oklahoma on May 11, 2023, about 10 minutes before a tornado hit the town.

## CHAPTER 8:

# RAINBOWS, FOGBOWS, AND SIGHTS IN THE SKY

Weather can be beautiful. The vibrant colors and delicate hues that appear in the sky are like artistic masterpieces. Sometimes, we just need to remember to stop and look for them.

Have you ever wondered what makes a sunset so stunningly red? Or how a rainbow gets its colors? Can rainbows happen at night? And what makes the air in the wintertime occasionally sparkle?

In this chapter, we'll learn all about **optical phenomena**—in other words, why you see what you see in the sky. We'll break down the science of sunlight, how it's responsible for all the different colors we see, and what happens when those colors combine and overlap.

At the end of the chapter, we'll work on an experiment together—creating our own rainbow. Of course, I can't promise you'll find a pot of gold—but you'll learn a lot on the way!

# WHAT COLOR IS SUNLIGHT?

**A**ll life on Earth depends on the sun. Without its brightness and warmth, Earth would be a cold, empty rock floating through space. Even from 93 million miles (150 million km) away, the sun's light is intense enough keep our planet a comfortable temperature.

But what *color* is the sunlight?

It turns out that sunlight is actually a combination of *every* color of light. All those individual colors are jumbled together. That produces *white* light. That's why sunlight isn't tinged blue, orange, or any other color. Since all the colors overlap, our eyes can't pick out individual shades.

Most of the time, we can only see the product—white light. Sometimes, however, that white light gets split up into component colors. That's the secret behind our blue skies or what makes a rainbow.

## DID YOU KNOW?

According to the Smithsonian Institution, the sun produces 3.85 septillion (10,000,000,000,000,000,000,000,000) Watts. If we could capture all the sun's energy for just one second, it could sustain the entire world's energy consumption for more than 4.1 million years.

If humans could harness all of this sunlight, we'd never need to turn to oil, coal, or natural gas ever again. The Earth receives more than 6,000 times more sunlight than we'd need to power every machine, house, and business in the world. The only problem? We can't easily collect all that energy. We would need to cover an area the size of New Mexico or Arizona in solar panels.

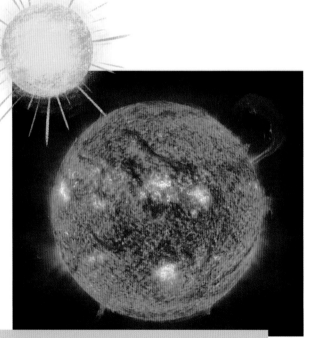

↑ The sun as captured from the European Space Agency's Solar and Heliospheric Observatory spacecraft.

## HOW POWERFUL IS THE SUN?

The sun is bright, and it's big. It's enormous, in fact. It's 109 times wider than the Earth. It would take 1.3 million Earths to fill the volume of the sun. And the sun is a giant nuclear power plant.

Chemical reactions fuse atoms together, releasing an incredible amount of energy. Those reactions take place in the sun's core, where temperatures can exceed 27 million degrees Fahrenheit (15 million degrees Celsius).

# IS THE SUN A RADIO?

Only a fraction of the energy emitted by the sun is light that we can see. We call that light the **visible spectrum**. All energy travels in waves. We can describe waves based on their **wavelength**, or the distance between two peaks in the wave. The entire range of all wavelengths is called the **electromagnetic spectrum**.

Visible light has a wavelength that our eyes are sensitive to. Colors like red and orange have longer wavelengths. Blue and purple have shorter wavelengths.

Some wavelengths are too *long* for our eyes to detect. Radio waves can range from a fraction of an inch to several miles (11 km) long. Though we can't see them, we can build antennas that do. That's how we can listen to the radio!

Microwaves are next on the spectrum—and yes, they are the same kind used in your microwave oven. Next up comes infrared wavelengths. Heat is a type of infrared wave. Then, we have the visible spectrum.

Above that, the wavelengths are too *short* for us to see. Ultraviolet, or UV, waves are an example. Have you ever gotten a sunburn? That comes from UV sun rays. They're absorbed by the skin.

X-rays are even more intense, with shorter wavelengths that can travel *through* our skin. That's how medical professionals are able to look inside your body and see your bones! Beyond that are gamma rays, the smallest waves on the spectrum, that are used to fight cancer.

The sun delivers energy of all wavelengths. Earth's atmosphere filters out most of the dangerous ones. As long as we apply sunscreen on days we're expecting to be outside, we're safe!

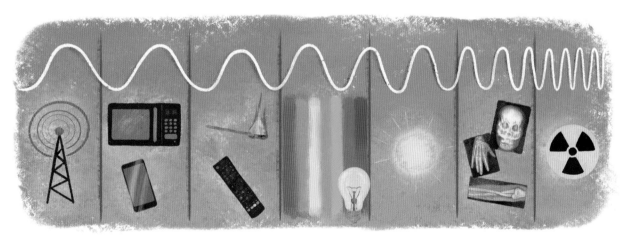

radio    microwaves    infrared    visible light    ultraviolet    x-rays    gamma rays

# WHAT MAKES A RAINBOW?

Rainbows form because of a different mechanism of splitting white light into colors. They're the result of **refraction**, or the bending of light.

When light enters a medium, like water, a crystal, ice, or anything else at an angle, it **attenuates**, or slows down. Different colors, or wavelengths, slow at different rates. That slowing results in refraction, or bending, of the light.

That's what happens when sunlight enters a raindrop. All the different wavelengths slow down and bend at slightly different angles. Since they no longer overlap, they don't combine into white light. Instead, they're split into individual colors.

Each of those colors bounces against the back of the raindrop and exits out the front. Then, the light returns to our eyes and violà! We see a rainbow.

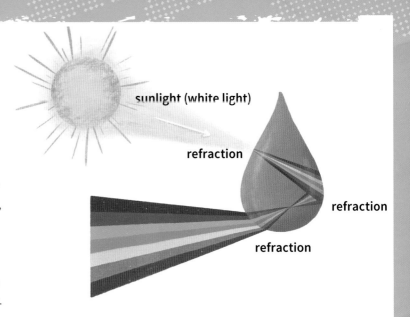

## WHAT ABOUT DOUBLE RAINBOWS?

Double rainbows occur when a fraction of the sunlight entering a raindrop bounces against the droplet's back wall a *second* time. That second reflection flips the order of the colors, so the secondary bow has red on the inside and purple on the outside. The secondary bow is also dimmer than the primary arc.

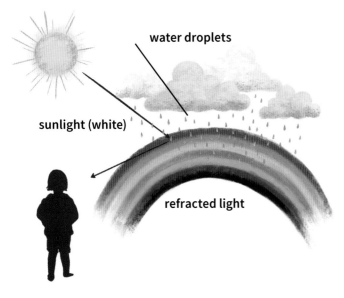

↑ To see a rainbow, turn your back to the sun and make sure the raindrops are in front of you.

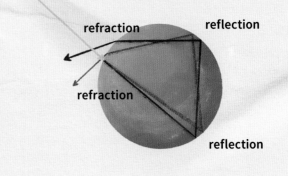

## ARE RAINBOWS REALLY CIRCLES?

Yep! Rainbows trace a full circle around the **antisolar point**—that's the imaginary point in the sky opposite to the sun. (If you want to get really technical, primary rainbows appear at a 42 degree angle out from the antisolar point, and the secondary bow, if there is one, forms 50 degrees outward.)

As long as the sun is above the horizon, the antisolar point around which the rainbow will form is usually *below* the horizon. That means that at least half of the rainbow, the part below the antisolar point, would be invisible to us. We only ever see the top half.

The highest, tallest rainbows form around sunrise or sunset, when the sun is low to the horizon. That's when we can *almost* see a perfect half-circle. (At that time of day, rainbows might be missing the green, blue, and violet colors. Since the sunlight is passing through the atmosphere at an angle, only the longer wavelengths, like red, orange, and yellow, make it through.)

So where can you see a circular rainbow? You have to be up high! Standing atop a mountain would do. Or flying in an airplane! Even being in a tall skyscraper might let you see the full circle of a rainbow.

↑ A double rainbow captured at a high elevation over Oplawiec, Poland on August 19, 2019. (Piotr Wieczorek via SpaceWeather.com)

## DO TRIPLE RAINBOWS EXIST?

Yes! So do quadruple rainbows (and even fifth-order rainbows). But, because of how the sunlight bounces through the raindrop, the third and fourth rainbows would appear on the *same side of the sky* as the sun. That presents a few challenges.

For starters, it would require rain clouds to be present to the left and right of the sun *but* not be blocking the sun. That sort of setup is difficult to achieve. Furthermore, the third-order rainbow would only be 24 percent as bright as a primary bow, and the fourth-order bow would shine only 15 percent as bright.

Assuming you, the sun, and the rain clouds are all in the right position *and* the super-rare third- and fourth-order rainbows have formed, you *still* probably wouldn't see it. Why? They appear around the sun. The bright sunlight would likely outshine them, making them difficult or near impossible to notice.

Only a few photos of third- and fourth-order rainbows exist. The first was taken on May 15, 2011, in southwest Germany. A photographer named Michael Grossmann used a tree to block the sun's most direct light. Then, he noticed a faint arc appearing in the sky exactly where the third-order rainbow was hypothesized, or believed, to exist. He snapped a picture—and it turned out he was correct!

Exactly a month later, another photographer—also in Germany—snagged a photo of a third- *and* fourth-order rainbow! They were too dim to see with the naked eye, but sensitive cameras and advanced processing revealed their presence.

In 2012, a fifth-order rainbow was captured. Humans will never be able to spot them visually, but as cameras become increasingly powerful, we're likely to document more examples. (The fifth-order bow isn't like other rainbows—it's broad and spread out, sitting in between the primary and secondary rainbows).

# MOONBOWS, FOGBOWS, AND MORE!

## MOONBOWS

It sounds crazy, but it's true! You *can* get a rainbow at night! They're not nearly as bright as their daytime counterparts, since the light comes from the moon. The moon phase needs to be full or almost full to be bright enough to spawn a moonbow.

↑ An incredibly rare *double* moonbow appears beneath the Northern Lights, or aurora borealis, over Stornoway, Eilean Siar, Scotland on November 7, 2017. (Giuseppe Petricca via SpaceWeather.com)

↑ A fogbow spotted on September 17, 2009 in the La Vérendrye Wildlife Reserve in Québec. (Claude Duplessis via SpaceWeather.com)

## FOGBOWS

Rainbows have ghostly white cousins called **fogbows**. They form the same way as rainbows, but instead of rain, they appear in fogbanks.

Fog is made up of tiny water droplets that are much smaller than raindrops. Because of that, sunlight passing through them doesn't get refracted, or bent, as much, and the colors don't split apart. That's why fogbows are *mostly* white, with only a bluish tinge on the inside and a hint of red outside.

↑ A fogbow over southeastern Massachusetts in October of 2022. (Nancy Franks)

## REFLECTED LIGHT RAINBOWS

Once in a while, "extra" rainbows can appear alongside a primary and secondary rainbow—and be just as bright. They're not triple or quadruple rainbows. Instead, they're **reflected light rainbows**.

Their formation requires a big shiny surface. You can't exactly find giant mirrors in nature, but a large, reflective body of water, like a calm ocean, lake, or bay can do the trick.

Reflected light rainbows aren't the reflection of existing rainbows, but rather rainbows that form from reflected *sunshine*. Sunlight shines onto the waters and then bounces skyward. A new set of rainbows—both the primary *and* secondary arcs—form around that upward-beaming sunlight.

↑ A reflected light bow captured on November 30, 2016. The extra bow likely stemmed from sunlight reflecting off the Columbia River, located near the Oregon-Washington border. (Chris Erikson via SpaceWeather.com)

↑ A supernumerary rainbow over northern Ireland on October 5, 2006. (Martin McKenna via SpaceWeather.com)

## SUPERNUMERARY RAINBOWS

Supernumerary rainbows resemble ordinary rainbows, but with extra repetitions of colors on the inside of the primary arc. A supernumerary rainbow might have three, four, or five miniature rainbows nestled within its inner edge. Next time you see a rainbow, look closely for a doubling, tripling, or quadrupling of colors.

They form when raindrops within a storm are mostly the same size. When multiple rays of sunlight enter each droplet, they take similar—but slightly different—paths and exit the raindrop a little bit misaligned. Upon exiting, those waves of light interfere with one another. That results in a pattern of light and dark bands, resulting in additional sets of colors.

# STORM CHASE ADVENTURES

## THE ARCTIC

The date was August 17, 2018. I was on a 420-foot (128-m) long ship called *The Healy*. It was a Coast Guard ice cutter built in the 1990s, designed to slice through 4½ feet (1.4 m) of solid ice when propelled continuously at a speed of 3 knots. I was volunteering for a cruise in the Arctic Ocean, assisting a team of 40 scientists conducting research on ecology, oceanography, and weather and climate.

We were around 72 degrees North latitude, or about 100 miles (161 km) north of the northern tip of Alaska, when a fog bank rolled in. The cold, frosty air was still. My breath was visible as I stood on the ship's eighth-floor observation deck.

I noticed the metal railings wrapping around the walkways were coated in a thin glaze of ice. "But it's not raining," I thought. I realized what was happening—we weren't just surrounded by fog, but rather *freezing fog*. That was depositing a slick rime, or frost, on exposed surfaces.

Freezing fog forms like ordinary fog, but at temperatures below freezing. The air has to be saturated, or holding as much moisture as it can. But if it's so cold, why don't the microscopic fog droplets turn into ice crystals? If the air is clean and pure, they have nothing to freeze onto—so they remain suspended in air as *supercooled* water droplets. That means they remain a liquid despite being chilled below freezing.

The sun shining through fog created a mystical scene as I glanced toward icebergs in the distance. "Wait a second!" I thought. "I should check for a fogbow." I walked to the opposite side of the ship, and there, splayed out before me, was the most magnificent fogbow I had ever seen.

A fogbow appears in the Chukchi Sea on August 17, 2018.

"*WOW!*" I yelled into the vast emptiness of the Arctic. The colorless fogbow appeared like a specter, as if plucked from an old-time black and white photograph. Since I was high above the water, almost the entire circle was visible. After a moment, I caught my breath, realizing how cold it was outside. I was in awe.

Something about the fogbow seemed odd though. I could just barely discern what looked to be an upside-down fogbow hanging from the inside of the main arc. It reminded me of a translucent hammock strung between opposite points of the primary fogbow. I realized what it was—an incredibly rare **reflected light fogbow.** It formed just like a reflected light rainbow.

In the middle of the fogbow at the antisolar point was a bull's-eye of rainbow colors, resembling an oil slick in midair. A **glory**!

# STORM CHASE ADVENTURES

## SPIKES OF LIGHT

In March of 2021, my adventure buddy Allen and I decided to fly to Fairbanks, Alaska. We were hoping to see the Northern Lights—the aurora borealis (see more on that in the next chapter!) While skies remained mostly cloudy, we did catch a brief glimpse of some green and pink aurora on our second to last night. On our final evening, we journeyed to the Chena Hot Springs—pools of warm, inviting waters in the middle of a snow-covered rock pile.

The drive back to our hotel after was long and sleepy. We narrowly avoided a moose in the roadway, missing it by just 2 feet (0.6 m). As we descended a hill into the city of Fairbanks, however, the scene looked otherworldly.

"Light pillars!" I shrieked, starling Allen, who had been asleep in the passenger seat of our rented van. Tall columns of luminance towered above every light on the ground. I immediately pulled to the side of the road, eager to step outside.

## KEY DETAILS

 **Location:**
Fairbanks, Alaska, USA

 **Date:**
March 2021

 **Type of Storm:**
Light pillars

↓ Light pillars over Fairbanks, Alaska on March 18, 2021.

"Diamond dust," I whispered gleefully as I slammed the door to the van shut. The air was glistening, as if glitter had been sprinkled from above. The air was *so* cold that any traces of moisture in the lower atmosphere were freezing, forming ice crystals.

I knew that the ice crystals had to be structured in the shape of flattened hexagons. These **platelets** were acting as little mirrors, reflecting distant light sources toward me. Each ray of light was bouncing off a crystal midway between the source and the observer (me), making the light appear to me as if it was coming from the sky!

↓ Light pillars as seen from the outskirts of Fairbanks.

↑ A shot of light pillars over a storage facility.

# HALOES, SUNDOGS, AND ARCS

Just like liquid raindrops can split sunlight into component colors, so too can ice. Before we learn about that, it's important to understand a bit about ice crystals in the atmosphere.

When water freezes into ice, its chemical properties cause it to form specific, predictable structures. We call these **ice crystals**. Some ice crystals are like long, hollow needles; others are platelets; and some look like more classic snowflakes. They always have either three or six sides. (At extremely low temperatures below -80°C [-112°F], however, ice crystals can form cubes.)

↑ An incredible assortment of haloes, arcs, and assorted optical phenomena captured by solar physicist David Hathaway at the Marshall Space Flight Center in Huntsville, Alabama on March 30, 2012. Cirrus clouds at the high altitudes fanning away from the remnants of Hurricane Sandy played a role in their formation. (David Hathaway via SpaceWeather.com)

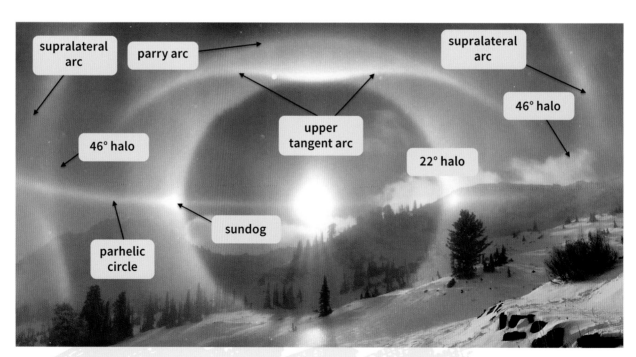

↑ An annotated view of a complex halo display captured at the Snowbasin Resort in Huntsville, Utah on November 25, 2018. Julie Morris was skiing at the time when she witnessed the display. (Julie Morris via SpaceWeather.com)

When sunlight enters these platelets, prisms, and other various shapes, it's refracted and again split into colors. The more complex nature of ice crystals compared to raindrops, however, makes for a wider variety of sky scenes, such as the following:

**Haloes** are rings around the sun. They form when sunlight passes through one of the lengthwise faces of a hexagonal prism ice crystal and then gets refracted before exiting. The light is bent 21.7 degrees, so the halo forms just under 22 degrees outward, surrounding the sun. (Other, rarer haloes can form 46 degrees outward from the sun. There are also various "arcs," or fragments of haloes, that appear when sunlight takes other paths through a hexagonal ice crystal.)

**Sundogs** appear to the left and right of the sun as bright splotches with some color. They form when sunlight enters through one side of a hexagonally shaped platelet. They can overlap with a 22-degree halo.

**Parhelic circles** are white lines that wrap around the sky at the same altitude as the sun. They are formed by sunlight reflecting off the vertical faces of ice crystals. Since the sunlight doesn't get refracted, or split into component colors, parhelia circles are white.

**Circumzenithal arcs** are rainbow-like curves that open around the highest point in the sky. They're formed when sunlight enters the hexagonal face of an ice crystal and exits a rectangular face.

**Sun pillars** are formed the same way as light pillars—horizontally oriented platelets of ice act as mirrors, beaming upward-aimed rays of light back toward an observer on the ground.

circumzenithal arc

supralateral arc

↑ Morris also snapped this photo looking upward. Ski resorts often manufacture artificial snow. The ice crystals are sometimes so "perfect" that a variety of haloes can form. (Julie Morris via SpaceWeather.com)

# MAKE A RAINBOW

**H**ave you ever wanted to make your own rainbow? Now you can!

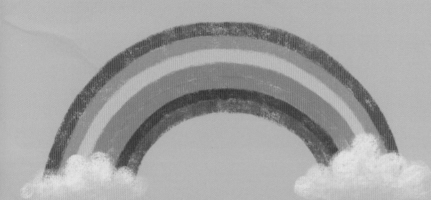

## THE SCIENCE BEHIND THE FUN:

Sunlight is reflected by the mirror through the water at an angle. All the different wavelengths, or colors, that make up the white light attenuate. Then, they refract, splitting into component colors. That's why you can see a thin rainbow on the wall.

## HERE'S WHAT YOU'LL NEED:

+ Small mirror
+ Drinking glass
+ Water
+ Sunlight

↓ High-energy particles from the sun can be dangerous to those of us on Earth. Fortunately, the Earth's magnetic field shields us from these particles, and dissipates that energy.

1. Fill the drinking glass about three-quarters of the way to the top with water.

2. Place the small mirror into the glass at an angle.

3. Place the glass near a window and tilt it so that sunlight striking the mirror is reflected against the wall.

4. Make sure the lights are off in the room and—aside from the window—keep the room as dark as possible. You should see a rainbow on the wall.

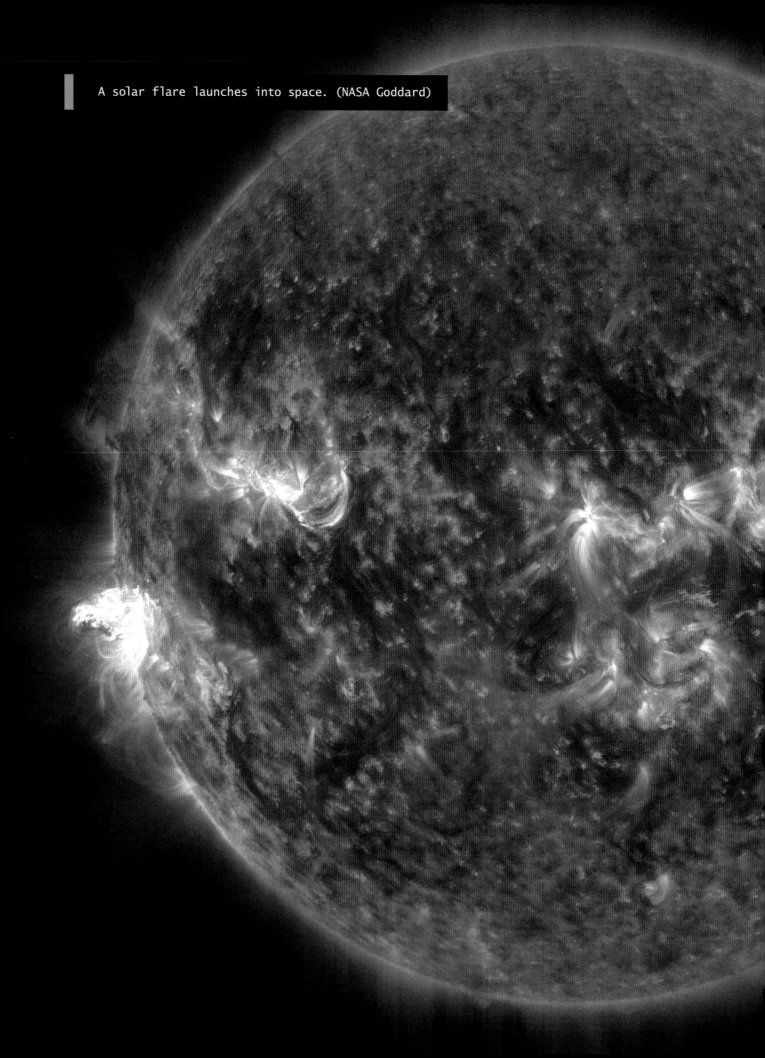

A solar flare launches into space. (NASA Goddard)

## CHAPTER 9:

# SPACE WEATHER

Have you ever heard of space weather!? Yep, it's a real thing—and **solar storms**, or storms from the sun, can hit us here on Earth! There's a whole team of special forecasters dedicated to predicting space weather. And their jobs are *very* important.

Space weather doesn't only happen on the sun. Other planets in our solar system experience storms too. Some have been raging for *hundreds* of years.

Other things that happen in space are more gentle and even sometimes beautiful. Eclipses happen when one planet or object passes in front of another. Once in a while, we get to see them here on Earth. Witnessing them can be life-changing.

In this chapter, we'll talk about "out of this world" weather—things that happen beyond our atmosphere. The goal is to learn a bit more about the Earth we live on and what happens beyond our world.

### DID YOU KNOW?

A giant high pressure system on Jupiter—known as the "Great Red Spot"—has been raging for at least 358 years. It produces wind speeds up to 268 mph (431 kph) and is 10,159 miles (16,349 km) wide—that's wider than the Earth!

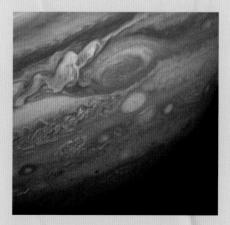

↑ The Great Red Spot as seen from NASA's Voyager 1 spacecraft in 1979. (NASA)

# SOLAR STORMS

The aurora borealis and the aurora australis, the northern and southern lights, are columns of light that dance in the night sky. They can turn the sky neon green, pink, or purple.

But how do the northern and southern lights form? They require a **solar storm**, or pulse of energy from the sun.

The core of the sun is incredibly hot—about 27 million degrees Fahrenheit (15 million degrees Celcius)! It's like a nuclear power plant. The unbelievable heat fuses, or attaches, atoms together. That releases a wild amount of energy.

Meanwhile, bands of magnetism wrap around the sun in horizontal belts. Within those bands, blobs of magnetic energy develop. Like bubbles in a lava lamp, they interact and interfere with each other. That produces regions of more chaotic, concentrated magnetism. Like bubbles in a pot of boiling water, they rise to the sun's surface. That forms **sunspots**.

Sunspots are cooler, darker regions that throb and crackle with magnetic energy. Some of that energy pours into space. Some energy loops back into the sun. We can't actually *see* the magnetism, but the solar plasma—the bright, luminous wisps of solar material trailing along with it—makes it possible for satellite cameras to spot it.

↑ A solar storm, or a **prominence** of solar material, on August 7, 2023. Captured by Dr. Sebastian Voltmer in Sardegna, Italy. (Dr. Sebastian Voltmer via spaceweather.com)

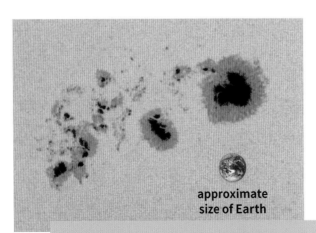

approximate size of Earth

↑ A giant sunspot, assigned the name AR1944, in January 2014, as seen by NASA's Solar Dynamics Observatory (SDO). (NASA/SDO)

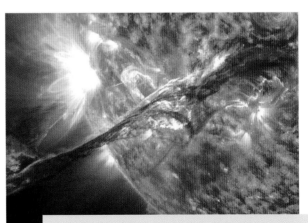

↑ A filament of solar material erupts from the sun on August 31, 2012. (NASA/Goddard Space Flight Center)

Once in a while, the interfering bands of magnetism in a sunspot interact explosively. That hurls a *burst* of energy into space.

That vigorous interaction first produces a brilliant flash of light. Scientists call it a **coronal mass ejection (CME)**. It ejects high-energy particles into space, traveling at the speed of light. If they're aimed toward Earth, they can disrupt GPS signals, spur shortwave radio blackouts, and cause problems for airplanes.

A coronal mass ejection contains magnetic energy, solar material, and high-energy particles. They ride a shockwave of sorts through space. If it hits Earth, the results can be memorable.

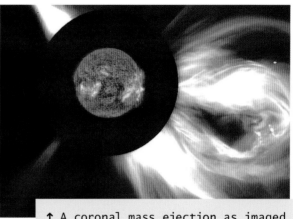

↑ A coronal mass ejection as imaged by NASA. (NASA/SOHO)

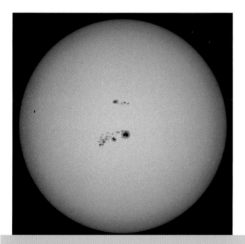

↑ Several sunspots imaged during the year 2000. (NASA/SDO)

That's because located at the center of Earth is a giant 750-mile (1,207-km)-wide ball of iron and nickel. Its edges are hot and gooey, like molten lava, so it can spin. It generates a magnetic shield around Earth.

When a CME hits, that magnetic shield protects us. It transforms that intense solar energy into visible light. That's what makes the aurora! It appears where the Earth's magnetic field is strongest—the north and south poles.

Ordinarily, the lights only stay high in the Arctic or Antarctic. Some parts of Norway, Sweden, Finland, and Antarctica can see them 50 to 100 nights a year. But if a CME is extra strong, it overwhelms Earth's magnetic field. That pushes the lights closer to the equator. Although rare, it's possible to see them in the United States, much of Europe, Asia, South America, and Australia.

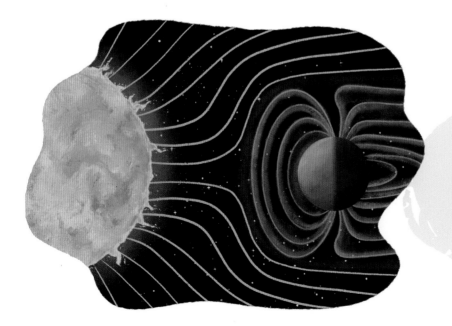

← High-energy particles from the sun can be dangerous to those of us on Earth. Fortunately, the Earth's magnetic field shields us from these particles, and dissipates that energy.

# STORM CHASE ADVENTURES

## CHASING THE NORTHERN LIGHTS

It was March 2021. My adventure buddy, Allen, and I had come up with a crazy idea: fly to Alaska. We wanted to see the Northern Lights.

One night, we were having dinner and decided to look online at flights. They were cheap! We looked at each other and smirked. "Are you thinking what I'm thinking?" I asked. He smiled and nodded. Five minutes later, we both had flights to Fairbanks, Alaska.

Fairbanks is 140 miles (225 km) from the Arctic Circle. But it's close enough that we'd have a shot of seeing the Northern Lights. Besides—we were going during mid-to late March. For reasons scientists still don't fully understand, the aurora is especially pronounced during the equinoxes. It's believed to be because of something called the Russel-McPherron (R-M) effect.

As soon as we landed in Fairbanks, the cold air took our breath away. It was 0 degree (-18°C)! Allen and I were too young to rent a car, but a moving company let us rent a cargo van. It was like driving a refrigerator!

Night after night, we drove through the frozen tundra looking for the Northern Lights. And every night we were disappointed—until the fifth night. After parking on a vacant road for hours, the sky exploded in color! Pinks, purples, and oranges swirled like glow-in-the-dark cinnamon buns in the sky. But by the time I set my camera up, it was over. The display disappeared as quickly as it came.

## KEY DETAILS

 **Location:**
Fairbanks, Alaska, USA

 **Date:**
March 2021

 **Type of Weather:**
The Northern Lights

↓ The Northern Lights over Canada from Alaska Airlines Flight 98 on March 20, 2021.

↑ A moose that Allen and I almost crashed into. (Matthew Cappucci)

## DID YOU KNOW?

Jupiter has its own version of the aurora! So does Saturn!

During the daylight hours, Allen and I spent our time adventuring. We rented snowmobiles, we drove to hot springs, and we almost crashed into a moose! Finally, on the last day, it was time to drop Allen off at the airport. He had a flight home at 6 p.m. I was taking a later flight in the middle of the night.

After saying goodbye to him, I sat at a restaurant, somber. I was lonely. Out of boredom, I began checking space weather data on my phone. Suddenly, I gasped. A solar storm was hitting Earth! Maybe I *would* see the Northern Lights after all!

Astronomers use a value called the **Kp index** to gauge if the lights will be visible. The higher the number, the more disturbed Earth's magnetic field, and the more people who can see the Northern Lights.

To spot them in Fairbanks, the Kp index has to reach a level 3. It was already at a 4! But it wasn't dark yet. My flight wasn't until 1 a.m., so I'd be stuck in the airport. And I didn't know where I'd be sitting on the plane.

To my surprise, the gate agent at the airport assigned me a window seat that was in an exit row. I'd have a front-row view if the lights were out there!

After a series of flight delays, we finally boarded the aircraft. It was 1:06 a.m. The sky was awash, polluted by city lights. The cabin dimmed and we took off into the night. The Kp index ticked up to a 6.

At first, the sky was absent of color. Then, the plane turned, and I couldn't believe my eyes. The sky was *filled* with green. The aurora looked like a curtain, with columns of green frosted in pink and purple. There were some aquamarine hues too.

The curtains danced and rippled, like laundry hung out to dry in a gentle breeze. Each column pulsated and flickered. The aurora moved quickly, as if trying to keep me entertained.

After an hour, the episode faded into the night. But the memories will last a lifetime. As the plane continued its nighttime flight, I sank back into my seat and fell asleep smiling.

# ECLIPSES

Eclipses happen when one planet or object blocks another. Here on Earth, we experience both solar and lunar eclipses.

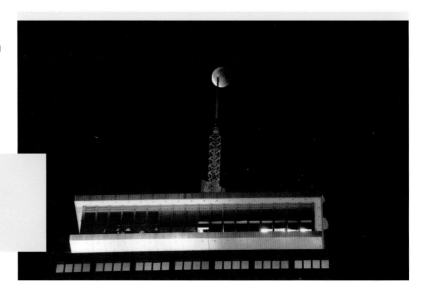

→ A total lunar eclipse hangs above the Prudential Tower in Boston, Massachusetts, on the night of September 27, 2015. (Matthew Cappucci)

## LUNAR ECLIPSES

**Lunar eclipses** happen when the Earth blocks the sunlight from reaching the moon, darkening the moon. Only a small amount of sunlight passes around the Earth—through our atmosphere—and reaches the moon, illuminating it. Since the light is filtered by our atmosphere, it turns red. Imagine the light from every sunrise or sunset on Earth projected onto the moon at once! Lunar eclipses happen about twice a year, and a **total lunar eclipse** occurs on average once every 2.5 years.

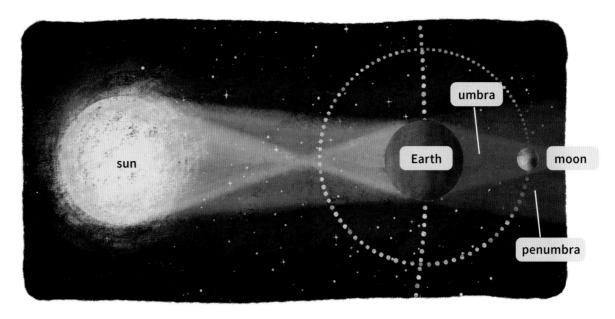

sun

Earth

umbra

moon

penumbra

# SOLAR ECLIPSES

**Total solar eclipses** are extremely rare. Any given place on Earth sees one every 375 years on average. The moon passes directly between the Earth and the sun, blocking the sun completely for a tiny slice of Earth's surface. That causes darkness to fall in the middle of the day. Day turns to night as the moon extinguishes sunlight. The moon's shadow, which might be only a few miles (kilometers) wide, is called the **umbra**.

Solar eclipses are spectacular. The fact that they exist is mind-boggling. The moon is 400 times smaller than the sun in width. But it's 400 times *closer* to Earth. That's why the two bodies look the same size in our sky—and why the moon can perfectly cover the sun. The longest a total solar eclipse can last is 7 minutes 29 seconds. Most only last seconds or minutes.

During the partial phase of a solar eclipse—when the moon only partially blocks the sun—people have to wear protective goggles or "eclipse glasses." If even a sliver of the sun is visible, its light can still damage your eyes! Only during totality—when the sun is fully blocked—is it safe to remove your glasses.

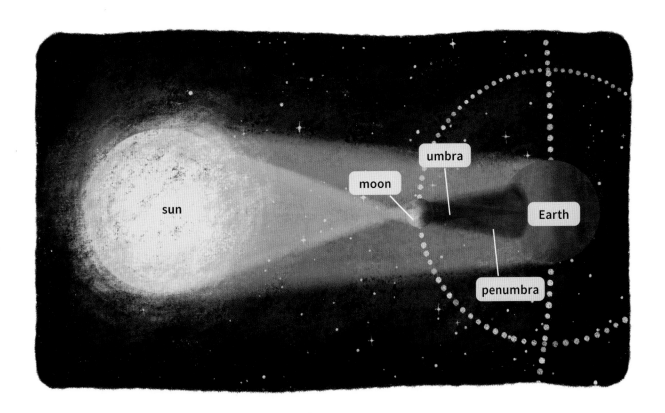

# STORM CHASE ADVENTURES

## SOLAR ECLIPSE IN CHILE

On August 21, 2017, a total solar eclipse transformed the early afternoon into twilight in a narrow swath across the entire United States. I stood in a field in Nebraska, awestruck as I gawked at the sky above me. My friend, Dan Satterfield, a TV meteorologist in Maryland, had journeyed there with me. Ten minutes after totality ended, he and I were still catching our breath.

"Ready for 2019?" I joked. He nodded.

"Absolutely."

The next solar eclipse would be on July 2, 2019. It would only be visible from Chile or Argentina—but I knew we had to go.

We both booked tickets. When the trip finally happened, he was delayed by two days. His plane had to land in Argentina, rather than Santiago, Chile, due to foul weather and fog.

On the day of the eclipse, we drove high into the mountains. We were near Vicuña, a tiny town in central Chile. Things were normal until about 10 minutes before totality. Then, the sky got weird.

Shadows seemed sharper. The sky looked dimmer. It was still daytime, but something felt strange. It was like looking at the landscape through a brown-tinged Instagram filter.

Then, the mountains to our west turned purple.

"There's the shadow!" I shouted. It was true—the moon's shadow was sweeping toward us at nearly 10,000 mph (16,093 kph). In just 30 seconds,

## KEY DETAILS

 **Location:**
Vicuña, Chile

 **Date:**
July 2, 2019

 **Type of Weather:**
A total solar eclipse

↓ A total lunar eclipse plunges the mountains of Vicuña, Chile, into darkness. (Matthew Cappucci)

↑ The diamond-ring effect moments before totality. The corona is visible too. (Matthew Cappucci)

↑ A partial solar eclipse in southern Chile on December 14, 2020.

## DID YOU KNOW?

Saturn has a jet stream around its north pole that's shaped like a hexagon!

↓ Saturn's jet stream. (NASA)

## ANNULAR ECLIPSES

An **annular solar eclipse**, sometimes called a ring of fire" eclipse, occurs when the moon is near **apogee**. That's the farthest point in its orbit around Earth. Since it's farther, it appears smaller in our sky, and can't fully block the sun. That leaves a ring of sunshine exposed.

the sky went from daytime to a deep blue azure. Stars awoke from their slumber and twinkled in the afternoon nightfall.

"Bailey's beads!" shouted Dan. He was right. Named after English astronomer Francis Bailey, this refers to the last pinpricks of sunlight that shine through the mountains and valleys of the moon, resembling a beaded necklace. The beads converged into one last glimmer of light—called the **diamond-ring effect**. Then, totality. We took our glasses off. I was speechless.

The sun had been replaced by a gaping black hole, like a void in the sky. It looked like a portal to another universe.

From behind the jet-black moon radiated the hair of an angel. That was the **corona**—the sun's atmosphere.

The corona is a region of plasma (the same glowing gas-like material in neon signs). It's superheated to more than 1.7 million degrees Fahrenheit (1 million degrees Celsius)! That's why it glows.

That solar material traces lines of magnetic energy surrounding the sun. That's how scientists can determine the magnetic structure of the sun.

Solar eclipses are the *only* time the corona is visible. Otherwise, the rest of the sun shines too bright for us to see it.

Most people never get to witness the corona. That's why traveling to see a total solar eclipse is so special.

↑ A "ring of fire" annular solar eclipse on October 14, 2023 in Albuquerque, New Mexico.

# METEOR SHOWERS

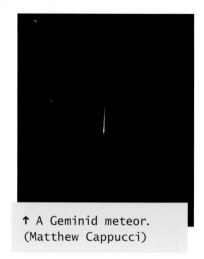

↑ A Geminid meteor.
(Matthew Cappucci)

Have you ever been driving down the road, only to have a bug go *SPLAT!* on your windshield? As you drive into the bug (or the bug flies into you), it leaves a smear on the glass. Gross!

That's how a meteor shower works. Meteors, or shooting stars, are small. They're only about the size of a grain of puffed rice. But when Earth plows through as we sail through space, the pebbles burn up in our outer atmosphere.

There are several clumps of pebbles in our solar system. Some are left behind comets and asteroids. Earth swings through the debris fields at the same time every year during our annual orbit around the sun. Each time we pass through a spattering of debris, we get a meteor shower.

There are three big meteor showers each year:

**The Quadrantids.** They peak in early January each year. Each Quadratid meteor shower moves through the atmosphere at 25 miles per second (40 kilometers per second)! Under a clear, dark sky, you might see 20 or 30 meteors per hour. The peak only lasts 8 hours, though.

**The Perseids.** The Perseids are perhaps the best meteor shower of the year. The debris comes from Comet Swift-Tuttle. The display reaches a maximum around August 12 or 13 each year. The Perseids are also rich in **fireballs**, or meteors brighter than the planet Venus! The peak lasts a couple days, and you might see 50 or more per hour!

**The Geminids.** They're around December 12, 13, or 14. Hourly meteor rates are similar to the Perseids, except the meteors move more slowly across the sky. And they're a bright green!

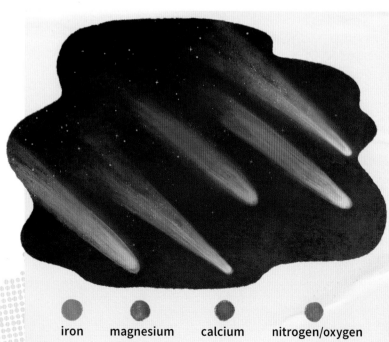

## WHAT COLOR ARE METEORS?

Meteors, or shooting stars, get their colors two ways. One comes from the compression of air in front of the meteor. The meteor moves *so* quickly through the sky that the air ahead of it can't get out of the way in time. That cushion of air heats it up so much that it glows!

The other way meteors get colors comes from their chemical composition. The meteor moves so fast that it burns up in the atmosphere, and the metals and compounds burn different colors.

iron    magnesium    calcium    nitrogen/oxygen    sodium

## HOW DO I SEE A METEOR SHOWER?

The more stars you can see, the more meteors you'll have a shot at catching! Just go outside and search for clear, dark skies. Find a place with a wide open view, away from trees and buildings—beaches, ball fields, and public parks are perfect spots. Turn off your phone screen and give your eyes a few minutes to adjust to the darkness. Then, sit back, relax, and enjoy the show!

↑ My friend Allen and I watched the Geminid meteor shower from the Atacama Desert. (Matthew Cappucci)

↑ An engraving by Adolf Vollmy illustrating the 1833 Leonid meteor storm.

## METEOR STORMS

On incredibly rare and unexpected occasions, an ordinary meteor shower can turn into a **meteor storm**. Meteor rates may top 1,000 per hour!

That happens when Earth encounters a particularly dense meteor stream. Imagine an entire swarm of insects all smacking into your windshield at once!

**The Leonids** are a November meteor shower that typically features a couple shooting stars per hour. In 902 BCE, astronomers in China and northern Africa reported meteors sparking in the night sky "like rain."

In 1833, it happened over the United States. A resident of Boston, Massachusetts, said the show resembled a snowstorm. The meteor storm lasted 9 hours and had rates as high as 240,000 meteors per hour—that's 60 a second! Another storm happened in 1966. Lesser, but still impressive, outbursts occurred in 1999 and 2001.

↑ A composite image from the Midcourse Space Experiment (MSX) satellite depicting Leonid meteors during the 1997 shower.

## DID YOU KNOW?

Some scientists believe that the extreme temperatures and pressures of both Uranus' and Neptune's atmospheres can crush carbon into diamonds. That means that it could actually rain diamonds!

# MAKE A PINHOLE PROJECTOR

The sun is the center of our solar system. Even though it's 93 million miles (150 million km) away from Earth (and 330,000 times heavier), it's powerful enough and bright enough to warm Earth and allow life as we know it to exist. But have you ever wondered what the sun actually looks like? This activity will enable us to answer that question.

## THE SCIENCE BEHIND THE FUN:

Of course, we can't directly observe the sun since it's too bright. But there are other ways to monitor it. The best option is to observe the sun indirectly.

Sunlight shining through a small-enough opening will cast a miniature likeness of the sun onto the ground below.

That's why we'll create a pinhole projector. By poking a small hole into a piece of paper, we'll make our own miniature projection system to generate our own image of the sun.

## HERE'S WHAT YOU'LL NEED:

+ Cardboard
+ White piece of paper
+ Aluminum foil
+ Scissors
+ Tape
+ Metal pin or paper clip

1. Cut a 2-inch by 2-inch (5-cm by 5-cm) square out of the center of your piece of cardboard.

2. Cut a 3-inch by 3-inch (8-cm by 8-cm) square of aluminum foil.

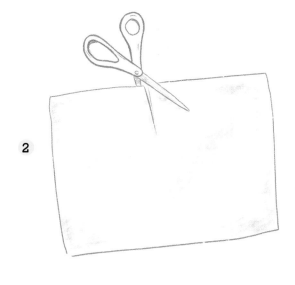

3. Use a pin or paper clip to poke a very small hole into the center of the aluminum foil.

4. Use tape to stick the aluminum foil to the cardboard. Make sure the small pinprick hole is centered inside the 2-inch (5 cm) "window."

5. Place the white piece of paper on the ground outside in direct sunlight. Hold your new pinhole projector several feet (2 m) over the paper. What do you see?

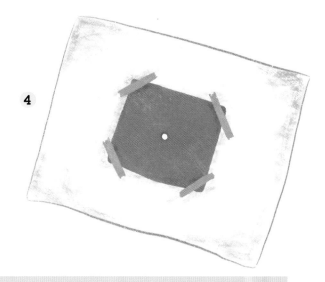

You should be able to see a miniature version of the sun projected onto the white paper. Maybe a few very tiny speckles—roughly the size of a pepper flake—appear. Those might be sunspots. (In order to see them, you'd have to have your projector far enough above the piece of paper to generate a sufficiently large image of the sun.)

During a partial solar eclipse, you can watch the moon block the sun. The image produced by your pinhole projector will start as a full circle and slowly morph into a crescent-shape. If you're watching a total solar eclipse, you can remove your eclipse glasses or goggles only during **totality**, when the moon fully blocks the sun.

## SAFETY TIP:

There are many ways to indirectly observe the sun. *You should never look directly at the sun, as doing so could cause irreversible damage or vision loss.*

To protect your eyes, consider either ISO-certified eclipse glasses *or* welding goggles of shade 14 or darker. Either option will allow you to look at the solar disk (the sun) while filtering out harmful ultraviolet and infrared radiation.

The Perito Moreno glacier is located in southwest
Santa Cruz province in Argentina. It's 19 miles
(30 km) long, and is one of 48 glaciers in
South America's Southern Patagonian Ice Field.
It's the third-largest reserve of fresh water
in the world. It's one of the few glaciers in
the world that, despite warming caused by the
changing climate, isn't shrinking—its mass remains
constant. This photo was takenfrom an airplane
flying to Puerto Natales in southern Chile in
December of 2021. (Matthew Cappucci)

# CHAPTER 10:

# CLIMATE CHANGE AND OTHER NATURAL DISASTERS

According to most estimates, the Earth is approximately 4.5 billion years old. Modern humans have only been around for 190,000 years or so—or just 0.00475 percent of Earth's history. During that time, temperatures have changed wildly. The climate, or average state of Earth's weather, has shifted a lot.

During parts of Earth's history, tropical trees bloomed in the Arctic. Other times, it was cold enough that snow and ice covered virtually the entire planet.

Over thousands of years, Earth's climate naturally changes. It always has and always will. But sometimes, human activity can influence or accelerate those changes. We can nudge Earth in a certain direction.

In this chapter, we'll learn about the different factors that shape Earth's climate. We'll discuss the difference between natural and human-caused climate change. We'll talk about how the changing climate affects the weather. And we'll examine other natural disasters too—like flooding and wildfires.

# WHAT IS CLIMATE?

The word *climate* describes the general state of the atmosphere. Usually, it's the average of 30 years' worth of collected data. Climate is different from weather. Weather is what's happening on short time scales, like from one day to another. Climate is very long term.

In other words, climate is what you *expect*, and weather is what you *get*. Think of it this way. Your *mood* is like the weather. It can change day-to-day. Sometimes, you're happy, and sometimes, you're angry. But your *personality* is like the climate. It's your overall disposition.

## WHY DOES THE CLIMATE CHANGE?

To answer this question, we have to remember what the *primary* driver of Earth's weather is—heat. Weather systems arise to balance **thermal energy**, or heat.

Heat primarily comes from sunlight, which warms the ground. Then, the ground warms the atmosphere. That's mainly what determines Earth's climate. It's also a product of how well the atmosphere is *holding onto* that heat.

So why would the Earth's climate change? Something would have to alter how much sunlight the Earth was getting *or* how good the atmosphere is at trapping heat.

Here are a couple things that can—and do—change Earth's climate:

**Earth's tilt on its axis.** Earth is tilted at 23.5 degrees on its axis. But over thousands of years, that number changes. It varies between 22.1 and 24.5 degrees during a 40,000-year cycle. That affects the intensity and distribution of sunlight on Earth. A greater tilt means more extreme seasons.

**Earth's distance to the sun.** Our orbit isn't a perfect circle. It's a bit elliptical, or oval-like. Right now, we're 3 percent closer to the sun in January than in July. That means we get about 6 percent more sunlight in January. Over 90,000 or 100,000 years, Earth's orbit changes from elliptical to a nearly perfect circle and back. Total incoming sunlight can change by 20 or 30 percent during that cycle. That can lead to wild changes in Earth's climate.

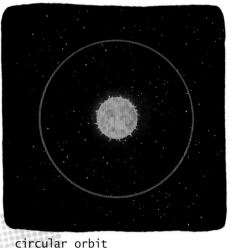

circular orbit

orbit with eccentricity

← Eccentricity describes whether a round shape is more symmetric, like a circle, or stretched in one direction, like an oval. A more eccentric orbit means a more elliptical, or oval-shaped, path.

**Precession,** or a wobbling of Earth on its axis. This is different from tilt. Precession is the *direction* of the tilt.

These three values undergo cycles. Since Serbian astrophysicist Milutin Milankovitch developed the theory behind the cycles, they're called **Milankovitch cycles**. Distance and precession can all overlap differently. That can produce many different types of climates.

There are also other things that naturally affect our climate:

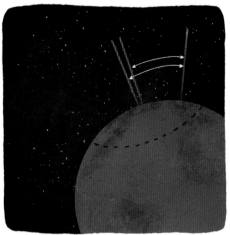

22.1–24.5° range of Earth's obliquity tilt

axial precessional movement

**The brightness of the sun.** The presence of sunspots affect how much **total solar irradiance (TSI)** is produced. That's a fancy term for brightness. Astronomers estimate that TSI varies by 0.1 percent during each 11-year sunspot cycle. The more sunspots, the more solar energy, and the more energy shined toward Earth. In the period between 1645 and 1715, known as the Maunder Minimum, hardly any sunspots were observed on the sun. Earth's temperatures cooled, and the Little Ice Age in Europe and North America intensified. There was also a slight decline in the number of sunspots observed in the early 1800s called the Dalton Minimum. Sunspots have been more common since 1950.

**How good our atmosphere is trapping heat.** We call this the **greenhouse effect**. If Earth had no atmosphere, all our heat would disappear into space. We'd be as cold and dead as the moon! We need *some* greenhouse effect to keep us a little warm. Too much, however, and we heat up uncontrollably. Carbon dioxide and water vapor, two types of greenhouse gases help us trap heat. If there's more of them, we get a warmer atmosphere. Conversely, volcanoes spew gases and aerosols that cool the Earth. In 1816, Earth's temperatures cooled 0.7 to 1°F (0.36 to 0.56°C) following the eruption of Mount Mayon in the Philippines in 1814 and Mount Tambora in Indonesia in 1815. That decrease in temperature caused widespread food shortages.

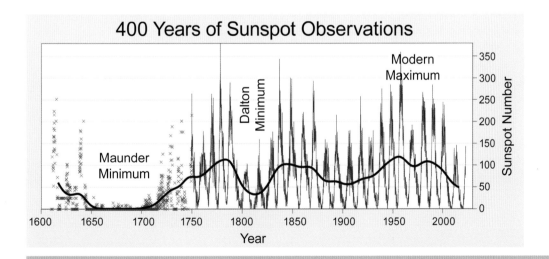

↑ A graph of monthly sunspot numbers showing the Maunder Minimum. During that time, temperatures on Earth were cooler for a variety of factors. The lack of sunspots probably combined with other natural factors to cause the Little Ice Age. So the Maunder Minimum was partially responsible, but so were other things. (Nils Simon, Wikipedia)

# HOW HUMANS ARE AFFECTING THE CLIMATE

Human actions pump greenhouse gases into the atmosphere. Every time you drive a car, use electricity generated at a power plant, or fly in an airplane, you're causing **emissions**. Emissions are substances that are released into the air, such as engine exhaust or greenhouse gases produced by chemical reactions.

There are more than 8 billion people on planet Earth. That means *a lot* of emissions. It's already changed the climate, and as the feedback mechanisms grow, we'll warm our planet even faster.

Since 1880, the world has warmed 1.9°F (1.1°C). The warming has sped up in recent years, especially since 1975. The past 9 years have been the 9 warmest on record. Humans have been keeping temperature records for about 140 or 150 years.

How do we know *we're* responsible for warming the climate? After all, the climate changes naturally, right? It comes down to *time scales*. Earth's climate has changed before—many, many times—but over thousands or tens of thousands of years. We're doing it on the scale of tens to hundreds of years. That's *much* faster. And it's changing the way we live.

We can also measure the amount of greenhouse gases we're emitting. Before the Industrial Revolution—when people began building machines—carbon dioxide levels sat around 280 parts per million, or PPM. That means that, of every million air molecules floating around, 280 of them were carbon dioxide. In 2023, we were approaching 420 parts per million.

Scientists have worked with politicians—the people who make laws—to help countries limit their emissions. Reducing how much carbon dioxide we add to the atmosphere will slow down Earth's warming. However, slowing our emissions will be difficult. That means slowing our warming will be too.

## DIFFERENT SCENARIOS FOR THE FUTURE

Using complex computer simulations, scientists have estimated four different possible scenarios for what might happen in the future:

### SCENARIO 1

▸ Completely eliminate greenhouse gas emissions by the year 2100.

▸ This is probably impossible to attain.

▸ Global temperatures would rise about 2°C (3.6°F).

### SCENARIO 2

▸ Emissions begin to slow by the year 2040.

▸ Warming of 3.6 to 4.2°F (2 to 2.4°C) would be expected.

### SCENARIO 3

▸ Emissions would begin to decline by 2045.

▸ Perhaps the most likely.

▸ In 2100, they'd be half of what they were in 2050.

▸ A warming of 2 to 3°C (3.6 to 5.4°F) would be expected.

▸ Numerous plant and animal species would be unable to adapt. They would go extinct.

### SCENARIO 4

▸ Emissions continue to build through 2100.

▸ Would be the worst.

▸ The planet would warm up to 4.8°C (8.6°F) and would look vastly different by the end of the century.

▸ Experts say this scenario is unlikely, but not impossible.

# HOW CLIMATE CHANGE AFFECTS THE WEATHER

The most notable change in the weather is something called **arctic amplification**. The poles are warming more quickly than the tropics. It's due in large part to the melting ice that's making the jet stream wavier and slower. That, in turn, makes for more extreme weather.

The wavy jet stream carries warm air masses all the way to the poles and frigid pockets of cold to the tropics or near the equator.

## FLOODING AND DROUGHT

Flooding and drought—two opposite things—can both be made worse due to climate change. How's that possible? It has to do with something called the **Clausius-Clapeyron equation**.

The equation says that, for every degree Fahrenheit () the air temperatures warms, the air can hold 4 percent more water. That doesn't mean it *does* hold more water, though. It depends on if moisture is available.

Where it is accessible, the atmosphere gets wetter. Storms transport more moisture and cause worse flooding. Rainfall rates increase, and individual downpours can be heavier.

But in dry environments, the hotter air evaporates more water from the ground. That *desiccates* (dries out) the landscape, allowing the air to heat up even more. It reinforces drought.

Here's an example. Sacramento, California, experienced 212 dry days in a row between March 20 and October 17, 2021. That was their longest dry stretch on record. Then, on October 24, 2021, they got 5.44 inches (13.82 cm) of rainfall—their wettest day in recorded history!

### DID YOU KNOW?

In the wintertime, it can be warm in places it usually wouldn't be. That can make more favorable conditions for tornadoes. Flooding can happen too. And—when the jet stream moves slowly—drought can last for a long time.

# CLIMATE CHANGE OR NOT?

There are some things we *can* firmly link to human-induced climate change. Other things we're not sure about. Bigger-scale phenomena are easier to tie to the warming world. Quicker or smaller things aren't.

## WARMER TEMPERATURES:

Extreme heat is becoming much more common than extreme cold. In fact, hot temperature records outpace cold ones 2 to 1. There is a firm link between a warming world and hotter readings.

## FLOODING AND DROUGHT:

Some parts of the world are drying out quickly. Others are getting wetter. Precipitation patterns can be strongly linked to human-caused climate change.

## CLIMATE-CHANGE AFFECTED

## SEA LEVEL RISE:

The melting Arctic ice is pouring more water into the ocean. That makes the water level rise. Water already present in the oceans expands a little bit too thanks to the warming. So, the sea levels are increasing. The National Oceanic and Atmospheric Administration (NOAA) and The National Aeronautics and Space Administration (NASA) estimate sea levels have risen 10 centimeters (0.4 inches) since 1993. Between 1901 and 2018, the sea level rose 15 to 25 centimeters (6 to 10 inches). That rise is getting faster. Sea levels could rise anywhere from 12 to 39 inches (0.3 to 1 meter) by 2100, depending on if humans cut emissions.

## HURRICANES:

The *number* of hurricanes isn't changing. But the *intensity* of tropical cyclones and hurricanes is. There has been an increase in the frequency of major hurricanes. Storms are also becoming wetter. Rainfall rates are 10 percent heavier. They're moving more slowly, dumping more rainfall. And they're more likely to rapidly intensify. Kerry Emanuel, a researcher at the Massachusetts Institute of Technology (MIT), estimates that, presently, a storm should strengthen by 70 mph (113 kph) in 24 hours just once per century. By the end of this century, it could happen every 5 to 10 years.

## WILDFIRES:

The warmer, and often drier, atmosphere is allowing wildfires to become more intense and common. Some are also growing taller. Record **heat domes**, or hot high pressure systems, are causing the landscape to dry out. That allows fires to become bigger. It's also true that humans are causing more fires. People build homes close together, and that makes it possible for wildfires to spread easier. And clumsy or accidental ignition, or lighting of fires, is common. It's not appropriate to fully blame fires on human-caused climate change.

## THUNDERSTORMS AND TORNADOES:

Experts are still struggling to understand how climate change is affecting thunderstorms and tornadoes. Some believe that hailstorms won't grow more *frequent*, but might produce *bigger* hail. The change in tornadoes is complicated. Since the jet stream is weaker, the wind shear might decline. That could mean less spin for storms and fewer tornadoes. But the wavier jet stream introduces warmer air masses in the traditionally cold season. That fuels thunderstorms, allowing tornadoes to occur in the wintertime. Overall, there probably won't be much change in the number of tornadoes annually. But peak season might be slower, while the winter becomes busier.

## RANDOM WEATHER CONDITIONS

## SNOWSTORMS:

Snow patterns are changing due to climate change. As the world warms, *less* snow is likely overall. But snowstorms are becoming bigger. Why? The air is holding more moisture. More storms are likely to end up as rain, cutting back on total snowfall. But, if it's cold enough to snow, the storms have more moisture to work with.

# SEQUESTER CARBON DIOXIDE

Plants are one of the biggest "sinks" of carbon dioxide. That means they take in $CO_2$, or carbon dioxide, and release oxygen. Since carbon dioxide is a greenhouse gas, that's a good thing. It's why protecting our forests is a great way to slow Earth's warming.

In this activity, we're going to make our own miniature ecosystem to sequester, or trap and store, carbon dioxide.

In other words, plants take in 6 carbon dioxide ($CO_2$) molecules and 6 water ($H_2O$) molecules each and transform them into glucose ($C_6H_{12}O_6$), food for the plants, and oxygen ($O_2$). That means plants literally clean the air! It's why lots of people want plants *inside* their apartment or home. It makes the air more pure and better to breathe.

## THE SCIENCE BEHIND THE FUN:

It's important to understand the chemistry of plants. They take in water and carbon dioxide, process it using sunlight, and produce sugar (glucose) and oxygen.

$$6\ CO_2 + 6\ H_2O + \text{sunlight} = C_6H_{12}O_6 + 6\ O_2$$

**(6 carbon dioxide + 6 water + sunlight = glucose + 6 oxygen)**

## HERE'S WHAT YOU'LL NEED:

+ **Empty soda bottle**
+ **An adult**
+ **Dirt**
+ **Grass seed**
+ **Flower seeds**
+ **Water**

1. Remove the label from the soda bottle. Take off the cap too.

2. Ask an adult to cut the bottle lengthwise, so there are two halves. Hold each one like a boat.

3. Fill each half with dirt.

4. Scatter grass seed throughout. Then, sprinkle a bit more dirt on top.

5. Poke your finger into the dirt to make 6 or 7 small holes. Pinch a few flower seeds into your fingers and drop them in each hole. Then, cover them once again with dirt.

6. Pour a bit of water into the makeshift planter.

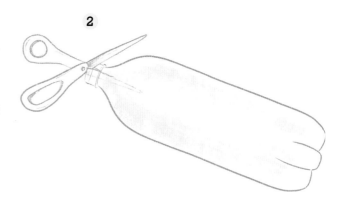

Over the course of 2 or 3 weeks, you should be able to see the seeds sprout and grow. The flowers will have roots that gather nutrients from the dirt. They'll combine those nutrients with water and sunlight to conduct **photosynthesis**, or the chemical reaction that produces plant food. The byproduct is oxygen, so the air inside your home will get cleaner. Just remember to keep the planter near a window. It needs sunlight! And don't forget to water it from time to time.

# ACKNOWLEDGMENTS

This book was made possible by so many people.

Tony Phillips at SpaceWeather.com graciously allowed us to print images shared by users of his incredibly popular educational site. Agencies like NASA and NOAA provided a menagerie of publicly available diagrams that we are able to share with budding scientists.

So many of the photos I've taken or trips I've written about have stemmed from adventures I've been on for the MyRadar app. Five years ago, when I embarked on a career in hopes of being a broadcast meteorologist, I always thought that weather apps were the competition; never would I have expected an app to become the model for what the future of weather broadcasting would be. Thanks to Andy Green, the mastermind behind MyRadar, we're able to bring viewers into the heart of every storm. We teach viewers something new every day, and I'm able to travel the country—and, once in a while, the world—doing what I love for an audience I love. A number of MyRadar adventures are included in this book, and we're just getting started.

Jason at The Washington Post always assigned me projects that taught me something new. The work and mentorship he's provided took me on a whirlwind tour of the world digitally, helping me grow as a forecaster and a writer. And Paul, who took a chance on me at FOX5DC in 2021—no matter what, I'll always be grateful for your years of teaching and creative freedom.

Appreciation is extended as well to all of my teachers over the years. They taught me how to teach—something that I've made central to my platform.

To my viewers, followers, readers and listeners: thank you. I can only do what I do because I have y'all along for the ride.

Thank you as well to the team at Quarto, including Gabrielle and Jonathan, for their tireless work on this project. And to Stephanie, who is an incredibly talented scientific illustrator.

And lastly, thank you to my parents and family—you gave me the best launch I could ever ask for. Now we shoot for the stars.

# ABOUT THE AUTHOR

Matthew Cappucci is an atmospheric scientist and meteorologist who lives in Washington, D.C. One of his first words was an attempt to say "wind meter," and he has loved the weather pretty much as long as he's been able to talk. He bought a video camera when he was seven years old to take videos of thunderstorms. After high school, he pursued an atmospheric sciences degree at Harvard and MIT.

When he graduated, he moved from Boston to Washington, D.C., where he worked as a weather writer at *The Washington Post*. Then he began working as a TV meteorologist. Nowadays, he can be found in newspapers, on TV, on the radio, and on the MyRadar app. He also makes frequent appearances on international TV outlets like DW News in Germany, SkyNews Arabia, or BBC World News. In his spare time, he works as an educational consultant.

When he's not working, Matthew is an avid traveler and storm chaser. He drives across the U.S. Great Plains chasing tornadoes every spring, flies into hurricanes during the fall, and visits South America or Australia each winter.

He is the 2023 FLASH National Weatherperson of the Year, and was nominated for an Emmy award in 2023 as well.

# ABOUT THE ILLUSTRATOR

Stephanie Hathaway is a Kansas City–area artist who specializes in creating educational content inspired by our natural world. She believes in using beautiful, dynamic illustrations to make learning about science and nature exciting and accessible to children of all ages. She is guided by the notion that many of life's valuable lessons can be learned from nature. It is her hope that her work will inspire families to explore and learn from the natural world right outside their own door. You can see more of Stephanie's educational nature-based studies and original artwork at stephaniehathawaydesigns.com.

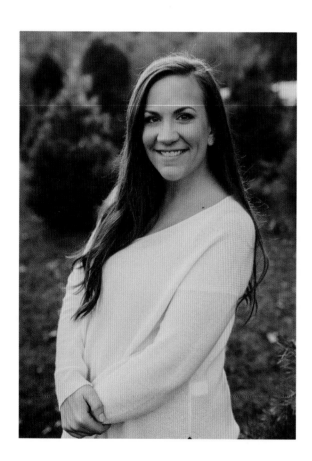

# INDEX